Battles in the Trenches

Battles in the Trenches

How Leaders in Academia Can Learn from Elite Athletes and Coaches

Perry R. Rettig with Darryl Sims

ROWMAN & LITTLEFIELD
Lanham • Boulder • New York • London

Published by Rowman & Littlefield
An imprint of The Rowman & Littlefield Publishing Group, Inc.
4501 Forbes Boulevard, Suite 200, Lanham, Maryland 20706
www.rowman.com

86-90 Paul Street, London EC2A 4NE

Copyright © 2022 by Perry R. Rettig and Darryl Sims

All rights reserved. No part of this book may be reproduced in any form or by any electronic or mechanical means, including information storage and retrieval systems, without written permission from the publisher, except by a reviewer who may quote passages in a review.

British Library Cataloguing in Publication Information Available

Library of Congress Cataloging-in-Publication Data

Names: Rettig, Perry Richard, author. | Sims, Darryl, author.
Title: Battles in the trenches : how leaders in academia can learn from elite athletes and coaches / Perry R. Rettig with Darryl Sims.
Description: Lanham, Maryland : Rowman & Littlefield, 2022. | Includes bibliographical references. | Summary: "This book examines lessons educational administrators (higher education and K-12) can learn about leadership, motivation, and organization from elite college, professional, and Olympic athletes and coaches"— Provided by publisher.
Identifiers: LCCN 2022013643 (print) | LCCN 2022013644 (ebook) | ISBN 9781475865004 (cloth) | ISBN 9781475865011 (paperback) | ISBN 9781475865028 (epub)
Subjects: LCSH: Educational leadership. | School administrators. | College administrators. | School management and organization. | Universities and colleges—Administration. | Sports—Psychological aspects.
Classification: LCC LB2806 .R439 2022 (print) | LCC LB2806 (ebook) | DDC 371.2/011—dc23/eng/20220617
LC record available at https://lccn.loc.gov/2022013643
LC ebook record available at https://lccn.loc.gov/2022013644

Trenches *is dedicated first and foremost to our mothers. M. Maxine Rettig and Mildred Elaine Sims continue to be sources of our inspiration and ground us in the reality of today's workplace. Sitting behind a keyboard can lead one to esoteric rhetoric. Speaking to one's mother can firmly ground an author's feet to a better sense of reality.*
This book has been written for those who aspire to roles of leadership. You will find an organization that often feels unnatural and unresponsive to its own people. Trust your senses and instincts. Trenches *is devoted to you. Hopefully, it will inspire you and support your intuitions about how to lead and how to support others on your team in their search for motivation and meaning. Hopefully, you will create and support more democratic values and principles in your organization and know your role within it.*

Contents

List of Figures	ix
Foreword	xi
Acknowledgments	xv
Introduction	1
1 Elite Leadership	7
2 Motivation at the Highest Level	31
3 Organization for Success	55
4 Putting It All Together	81
Bibliography	105
Biographies	109
About the Authors	115

List of Figures

Figure 1.1	Supervisory Continuum	11
Figure 1.2	Johari Window	12
Figure 1.3	Leadership Styles	12
Figure 2.1	Professional-Bureaucratic Matrix	34
Figure 2.2	Mintzberg's Professional Bureaucracy	35
Figure 2.3	Maslow's Needs Hierarchy	35
Figure 2.4	Porter's Work Needs Hierarchy	36
Figure 2.5	Maslow's Final Needs Hierarchy	38
Figure 2.6	Maccoby Leader/Led Motivation	38
Figure 3.1	Dolan's K-12 Education Governance Model	57
Figure 3.2	Higher Education Governance Model	58
Figure 3.3	Ecological Pyramid Model	60
Figure 3.4	Higher Education Organizational Pyramid Model	60
Figure 3.5	Ecological Pyramid Model with Checks & Balances	62
Figure 3.6	Higher Education Organization Model with Checks & Balances	62
Figure 3.7	Cerroni Adaptation of Leadership/Motivation "Target"	76
Figure 4.1	Leadership Congruency Model	102

Foreword
N. Karl Haden, PhD

For millennia, sports have served as a metaphor for leadership, team performance, and life in general. With interviews of nearly forty elite athletes and coaches, Perry Rettig and Darryl Sims take us behind the analogies and into the minds and practices of people who are exceptional at what they do. The premise of *Battles in the Trenches* is that leaders in educational and corporate institutions can learn valuable lessons from elite coaches and athletes. The authors have traded their jerseys for coats and ties, but they write as former elite athletes, past football coaches, and now accomplished leaders in higher education. They are uniquely qualified to explore how leadership in athletics is transferrable to other environments.

I have spent my career developing leaders in higher education, with an occasional detour through the business world. Most of my work is with those who teach and lead in schools and colleges of the health professions. I feel a sense of calling to my vocation, something I was born to do. Whether consulting with a college administrator or facilitating professional development programming, many of these individuals have not one, but two doctorates along with other graduate degrees. I have the privilege of engaging with people who define and exemplify excellence. While they are not athletes, they are elite in their fields. Thinking of the thousands of leaders and faculty members I have encountered through the Academy for Advancing Leadership, I am compelled to use a sports metaphor. At my best, I am a coach to people whose talents exponentially exceed my own.

Whether one is an executive, teacher, doctor, athlete, artist, or contributor to another vocation, the highest levels of performance are the result of many things—genes, connections made along life's way, and good fortune, among others. Woven through these influences is assiduous practice. While the star guard makes a three-pointer look almost effortless, the spectator does not see the thousands of shots, including countless bounces off the rim, that fine-tuned the senses and motor skills. The best teachers are lifelong learners, perfecting not only their knowledge of the subject matter but also their understanding of students and their practice of pedagogy and andragogy. While their methods may vary, the greatest leaders are relationship builders and skilled communicators. Whatever the game, the business, or human endeavor for good, the elite have made excellence a habit in what they do.

My personal views on leadership development are oriented around the concept of excellence as a habit and significantly influenced by Aristotle. Over two thousand years ago, Aristotle discovered that excellence is internal to a discipline or field. He observed athletes, politicians, teachers, and elite practitioners of different disciplines and recognized how deliberate practice of the rules that define the discipline leads to superior outcomes.

Rules are both formal and informal. For example, the game of football has a codified set of rules but playing the game teaches unwritten rules and provides insights about such matters as reading what a defender is likely to do before the ball is snapped. Exceptional leaders are experts in applying the rules of communication, many of which are learned in formal instruction or written into policies. However, the exceptional leader has also developed a sixth sense to read the room or intuit what is unsaid in a negotiation. Aristotle's notion of internal excellence is close to the contemporary understanding of competencies: the knowledge, skills, and attitudes—defined within the game, profession, or discipline—for successful practice.

Aristotle's work may serve as a precursor to contemporary discussions of competency, but his unique contribution to our understanding of excellence is not about what the elite do. He wrote that excellence is a state of character concerned with our choices. By asserting that excellence is a state of character, he turns our attention away from what one does to who one is. If we apply this reframing of excellence to leadership, the fundamental question, the prerequisite consideration, is not "What should I do?" but rather "What kind of person should I be?"

If our state of character is concerned with our choices, then the choices we make are of no small consequence. Leaders are judged by their decisions more than anything else. Repeated choices or actions become habits. Habits that are good for us and those around us are virtues. Those that harm us and others are vices. Elite leaders, whether in sports, business, education, or elsewhere are exceptional at what they do, but the wellspring of their competence is character. These character strengths or virtues include such traits as courage, humility, fairness, hope, and wisdom. Leaders with these character strengths are virtuous leaders.

Rettig and Sims illustrate the centrality of character again and again throughout *Beyond the Trenches*. Quoting the NFL coach Chan Gailey in chapter 4, "[The best leaders] are people of great character. Lots of people can be 'successful,' but the persons of great character are the great leaders." The reader sees character in the love that coaches express for players, in the perseverance required to overcome personal hardships on the way to becoming a professional athlete, and in the trust that is the foundation of the coach-player relationship and team performance. Just as coaches create an environment where players can grow their talents and play at the highest levels, virtuous leaders create organizations where people can flourish—where they have the freedom to actualize their unique talents, the opportunity to develop their potential, and the chance to contribute to a purpose that transcends self-interest.

We learn from coaches and players interviewed in *Beyond the Trenches* that how you play the game matters but so does winning. Without wins, a team cannot build its capacity to become even better. Without profit, a corporation cannot innovate, support employees, and make their communities better places. Without high achievements in education, research, and service, higher education institutions cannot attract students, faculty members, and external support required for discovery and the generation of new knowledge. Winning, profit, and prestige are not the end but a means to the end of human flourishing.

Many books on leadership tilt either to anecdote or to abstraction. The authors have balanced theory and practice to create an approachable guide to improve one's leadership. Through the lives and testimonies of elite athletes and their coaches, Rettig and Sims establish that exceptional leaders possess not only the competencies to lead but also the character to lead. They prove the premise of the book: leadership lessons from the highest levels of athletics transfer, without reinterpretation or resorting to metaphors, to educational institutions and business.

Acknowledgments

As with any team endeavor, *Trenches* owes its existence, and any success it has, to the efforts of many people.

Dr. Karl Haden's insights have been invaluable as the seeds to this project. It was obvious from the outset he needed to write the foreword for this book. His experience and knowledge provide an erudite analysis with an eye toward the future.

Cindy Tinius has served as the team support staff throughout. Her tireless behind-the-scenes work and support must be recognized and have always been greatly appreciated.

All those friends, both new and old, who helped us through their interviews and insights, and by helping us to make connections with their associates, made this all possible. In this regard, *Trenches* has been organic. A few strategic contacts grew into others. Soon, the contacts blossomed into a beautiful mosaic—apologies for mixing the metaphors. This book is built on the energy of these emerging organic connections. We must acknowledge so many tremendous and eager participants to this team endeavor.

Introduction

It was the first night game of my sophomore year on the team. I was collecting splinters on the bench when our star defensive end received a terrible knee injury. Our coach turned toward the bench, and I urgently leaned forward. Our eyes locked onto one another.
   The coach shouted, "Rettig!"
   I cried back, "Yes, coach?"
   He said, "Sit back; I can't see everybody!"
   You will never know if that is a true story, but you can be assured that the rest of the stories and anecdotes in the *Trenches* are true. They come from some of the current and past elite athletes and coaches in collegiate, professional, and Olympic sports.
   Leaders, by their very nature, are storytellers. They have life experiences, vision, and drive. They know where they want to go and how to get there. They model, motivate, and inspire others to collectively achieve a common purpose. We have found that many elite coaches and athletes exhibit tremendous leadership skills—attributes which can be shared with educational and even corporate leaders.
   This book is shaped by three main foci: leadership, motivation, and organizational structure—each with a chapter devoted to it. The first three chapters are a lay of the land that begin with a review of the literature. The research provides a framework for a series of interview questions about the topic at hand. Each chapter concludes with a compilation of thoughts and anecdotes from these coaches and athletes.
   Chapter 1 focuses on what makes a successful leader. Chapter 2 is devoted to understanding the concept of motivation. Chapter 3 describes organizational and structural concepts of our institutions. Chapter 4 pulls the previous three chapters together. It begins with a review of what we've been

told and then follows with some final leadership perspectives from these interviewees. The chapter concludes with the painting of a mosaic of lessons we can learn and reflect upon for our own careers. This mosaic is pulled together neatly in a new Leadership Congruency model.

While each of the three primary foci (leadership, motivation, and organizational structure) is discussed in isolation, their real-life interplay every day is dynamic and seamlessly woven together. We use Douglas McGregor's Theory X and Theory Y[1] as the umbrella concept under which these three topics fall. These competing dualistic themes form a mental construct for how all leaders, whether they realize it or not, view their employees. In turn, how leaders lead, approach motivation, and structure their organizations should, theoretically speaking, be congruent. It is our speculation that more often than not, leaders feel a sense of incongruency.

A cautionary note is appropriate at this time. The reader will find we use the terms "professionals" and "bureaucrats" often throughout this book. The use of these words is very purposeful, and their definitions must be precise. Professionals are highly trained, skilled, and experienced individuals with a particular set of ethics to which they are beholden. Professionals have both an artistic and a scientific approach to their work.

Bureaucrats are not meant in any sense as a derogatory or spiteful term. Bureaucrats have their own set of skills and training which are standardized and routinized. Leaders create change, and they hire bureaucrats to manage the change. Most of us have held bureaucratic obligations and responsibilities throughout our careers. Workers within a bureaucracy play critical roles to the success of every organization, but they must not usurp the role of the leaders or the professionals. Nuanced discussions will follow later.

The interviews are based upon a series of questions that have emerged from an examination of the literature on the three main topics or foci. Nearly forty elite coaches and athletes have been interviewed, and their stories and reflections are told here. An excellent cross-representation of men and women from a wide breadth of athletics share their insights and experiences. Former Olympians, and other athletes and coaches from Divisions I, II, and III, and coaches and players from the NFL, NBA, and MLB took part.

A final note on a hidden agenda item that has haunted the authors for decades. We are all more than familiar with the mythic stories and tales of the heroic leaders in athletics. These are the legends of Vince Lombardi and Knute Rockne, and the determined and self-demanding Jim Thorpe and Jackie Robinson. Are these more the rule or the exception? Is the vast field of athletics a fair model for executive leadership in educational or even corporate settings? Or is athletics so unique, perhaps like the military, that comparisons and transferability simply are inappropriate?[2]

Perhaps the legendary leaders of lore are more myth than reality. The John Wayne persona might be more a fabrication of Hollywood, or in the case of athletics—more a case of slick marketing or a very narrow slice of Sunday afternoon sideline behavior. But these scenes are miles away from reality. The coaches and athletes interviewed seem to think so. They know what the television cameras reflect for our viewing is not an adequate representation of the people behind the game.[3] What we see is not the full reality, but in some instances, it has become our model, and that is a shame.

Sports columnist for the *Washington Post*, Sally Jenkins explained, "Miami Heat President Pat Riley wrote about this leveling dynamic in his autobiography: 'This is what happens whenever people on a team decide not to trust. Everyone will gear down their effort until they're doing just enough to get by.'" Riley concluded, "But the opposite happens when the leader is a genuine collaborator. Teammates gear up."[4]

Jenkins later described Dan Campbell of the Detroit Lions—at a press conference. "'Compatibility is important,' Campbell said. 'It's highly important. It doesn't matter—you can put the best coaches in the room, and if they're all a bunch of alphas, and they're trying to eat each other alive, you're never going to get anything done. . . . It's a collaborative effort; it's give-and-take.'" "It works because the very best coaches don't tell people what to do. They ask them what they want to do together."[5]

Finally, are our beliefs about approaches to leadership, and to motivation, and how we structure our organizations congruent with one another or do they misalign and fight one another? In other words, do our models fit our beliefs? Do we lead, motivate, and organize in ways that support what we believe about our professional colleagues? These are the hidden questions we hope to reach by the book's end.

THE AUTHORS

Perry and Darryl arrived in one place through very different journeys. Our backgrounds may have been varied, but we came together for a love of leadership and a love of football. The place was the University of Wisconsin Oshkosh—a state comprehensive DIII school of about 13,600 students.

At the time, Perry was serving as associate vice chancellor for Academic Affairs and maintained his faculty credentials as a tenured full professor of Educational Leadership and Administration. He was born and raised in the Midwest and had recently finished playing semi-pro ball for the Fox Valley Force as defensive end. Now, he extended his association with football as a volunteer assistant defensive line coach for the University of Wisconsin Oshkosh Titans.

Darryl was born in North Carolina and raised in Bridgeport, Connecticut. Eventually, he attended college in Madison, Wisconsin, where he starred on the Big Ten Badgers football team as a defensive tackle and majored in Speech Communication. Darryl later earned a master's degree in Educational Leadership and Administration. He went on to have a stellar career in the NFL on the Pittsburg Steelers and Cleveland Browns. A knee injury finished his playing career. After coaching stints in the NFL and NFL Europe, Darryl eventually moved back to Wisconsin and became athletic director and assistant chancellor at University of Wisconsin Oshkosh.

It was on the football field sidelines and locker rooms where we became friends and colleagues. We may have had different journeys, but we shared more similarities than differences, and we came together for a common goal and purpose. For a moment, a personal anecdote might help to establish some context for this book.

PERRY RETTIG'S ESSAY

Let me begin with a short story of my time playing semi-pro ball:

A searing hot bolt of electricity shot through my head as I crashed into the ground. On my back, I looked into the afternoon sky and saw nothing. Literally, nothing, only blackness. I reached under my facemask as I was certain my eyes had popped out of my skull. But my fingers touched my staring eyeballs. For an eternity of thirty seconds this was my reality. Then, everything slowly came back into focus.

This was just one of numerous hits, separate stories if you will, in my experience playing semi-pro football. My experiences are not unusual to any of this brotherhood who has played semi-pro ball. We lifted weights and ran sprints and distances on our own time. We practiced together as a team twice a week and played games on Saturday afternoons, and then we went to work at jobs as varied as our diverse teammates. At work people would ask any of us, "Are you hurt?" The quick retort was always the same, "If you're not hurting, you're not playing."

We had an interesting mix of characters in our huddles. In the offensive huddle, we had Griff—our QB who played preseason ball on an NFL team in the NFC South Conference. Willie played running back in the Big 12; Fish was a chiropractor and had played FBS ball; Caleb played in NFL Europe; Ryan was a sheriff deputy; and, Travis—well, Travis knew Ryan on the other side of the bars. He came to more than one practice with an ankle-monitoring brace.

We called ourselves on the defense, "The Dark Side." Our star cornerback played in the NFL's NFC North for three years. Two linebackers were vets of the Gulf War, and several others played NCAA Division I, II, and III ball. The centerpiece was our nose guard. "House" was 6'11" and 470 lbs. At forty-two, I was the old guy and started at defensive end. I was the only one among the team who had a PhD, was a former school principal, and was now a college professor.

These we had some of the best times in our lives. While we came from all sorts of backgrounds, and likely wouldn't always socialize off the field, when we were on the field, we were all together. We were tight and took care of each other. We toiled together through miserably hot and sweaty practices, pushed each other through unpleasant conditioning drills, traveled on the road together, and won the league championship.

Through my time with this team, I learned many lessons. I can sit at a meeting at work and recognize those who have played team sports or were members of a musical or theatrical ensemble. These people know how to play a role and how to come together to work toward a common goal. They know they can only be successful when each member plays a valued part, and they will not let their colleagues down. They put in their time, often quietly behind the scenes, because they know the value they bring to their team.

My third and final season was cut short in a practice. On that ever-so-vivid play, I shot across the line only to turn to my left and see Dan a split moment before his helmet hit me in the neck and his shoulder into my clavicle, tearing it away from the joint. It was one of those hits we all worried about, one that would keep you from work the next day, and it meant I needed to hang up my cleats, one final time.

Would I do it, again? In a heartbeat. "Darkside!"

*This appeared in the *Atlanta Journal-Constitution* on February 3, 2020.[6] Perry described the time he spent playing semi-pro football and the life lessons he learned.

After graduating from college with a bachelor's degree in education, I served as a public school teacher for five years and then as a public school principal for seven years, all in the state of Wisconsin. It was during these formative years I earned both a master's degree and a PhD in Educational Leadership and Administration. I then became a professor of Educational Leadership and Administration in South Dakota's Northern State University for a year before returning to Wisconsin to again serve as a professor. Eventually, I advanced to serve as associate vice chancellor for Academic Affairs for a total of seventeen years at UW Oshkosh.

In 2013, I moved to Georgia where I became vice president for Academic Affairs and then as vice president for Enrollment Management and Student Affairs at Piedmont University for the past eight-plus years. In the meantime, I have also served in dual capacities as vice president for the Athens campus, and as interim deans for the School of Nursing & Health Sciences and School of Education. Finally, I have retired from those senior leadership roles and now serve as distinguished university professor and teach tomorrow's leaders.

It was during my time as associate vice chancellor for Academic Affairs at the University of Wisconsin Oshkosh when I played semi-pro ball for over two years before a shoulder injury forced me to hang up my cleats. I was in my mid-forties. It was during these days I made my acquaintance with Darryl Sims.

Darryl and Perry have been brought together by circumstances. These circumstances come from a love of education and athletics and a drive to lead others toward a common vision. From our work on *Trenches*, a number of our assumptions about athletes have been affirmed, yet others have challenged and surprised us. While there never was complete unanimity in any of the experiences of these coaches and athletes, certain themes clearly emerged time and again. The stories are impactful, relevant, and transferable to every leader no matter the field.

Let us share.

NOTES

1. Douglas McGregor, *The Human Side of Enterprise* (New York: McGraw-Hill, 1960).

2. Perhaps we don't want to know. At the time these interviews have been compiled, the NFL has seen two head coaches fired in mid-season (Jon Gruden and Urban Meyer). Multiple cases of criminal charges against current and past athletes are in the courts on a weekly basis. Professional sport team owners sell and move their franchises with little sense of the impact on their communities. The International Olympic Committee and nations seem at political odds.

3. Vince Lombardi himself, as well as those who knew him best—fellow coaches and players, have painted a very different portrait of the legendary field leader. He was personally driven, intelligent, and mission-driven, but he often questioned himself, individualized his approach to each of his players, and respected the dignity of their professional ethic. Such stories are made clear in his own book and that of his biographer, listed below.

    Lombardi, Vince, and W.C. Heinz, *Run to Daylight* (New York: Prentice Hall, 1967).

    Maraniss, David, *When Pride Still Mattered: A Life of Vince Lombardi* (New York: Simon & Schuster, 1999).

4. Sally Jenkins, "Keys to Good Coaching," article in the Washington Post (Carried in the *Atlanta Journal-Constitution*, December 26, 2021), 42.

5. Jenkins, "Keys to Good Coaching," 42.

6. Perry Rettig, "Taking His Hits with Playing Semi-Pro Football," Article in the (*Atlanta Journal-Constitution*, February 3, 2020), A5.

Chapter 1

Elite Leadership

It is better to be feared than loved if one cannot be both.[1]

Is this quote from an aspiring Machiavelli to the new prince the best we can hope for in leadership? Do the best leaders use a manipulative combination of love and fear to lead others? Is fear the penultimate tool of effective leadership? What does the literature tell us? What do some of our elite coaches in athletics tell us?

THE LITERATURE

There are dozens if not hundreds of books describing leadership in its broadest senses, as well as those focused exclusively on both K-12 and higher education. These books range from the prototypical textbook describing varied models and theories of leadership to those which describe model leaders who have been deemed worthy of our study. The subsequent questions then become, "Are leaders born, or are they made?" "Is it nature or nurture?" Or "Is leadership more of an art or a science?"

Members of the academic community focus on theoretical models for understanding leadership. Such models are descriptive of the traits our leaders possess, or the processes they wield to help to conceptualize these distinctions.[2] Traits or innate characteristics would lend themselves to a natural or even an artful understanding of leadership. Skills and processes follow from a nurture or scientific inclination. Still other models target on the locus of the leader's authority or the behaviors of their followers. The following pages will provide a cursory view of the literature for each of these perspectives.

Before describing how individuals become leaders, it is worthwhile to differentiate between the responsibilities of leaders and managers. Professor John Kotter describes in detail the domains of each position. Leaders are hired to create change, and they hire managers to implement and enforce the change. According to Kotter, leaders establish direction, align people, and motivate and inspire their workers.[3] Managers, on the other hand, are responsible for planning and budgeting, organizing and staffing, and controlling and problem-solving. Leaders create change; managers maintain stability. This focus on skill sets and functions of administrators lends itself more to the conceptualization of leaders being made, rather than born.

With this context established, do we consider coaches to be leaders or managers? Do they try to create change or maintain the status quo? A nuanced answer is likely necessary. Similarly, the reader should ask themselves if they are serving in, or aspiring to be in, a leadership or managerial role. It should be noted that for purposes of this book's discussion, the term "bureaucrats" will be used from time to time. This term should not be considered libelous in the least. It simply refers to highly trained employees tasked with carrying out prescribed managerial responsibilities, not unthinking automatons.

Just as it is important to differentiate between leadership and management, so too it is important to describe the differences between power and authority. Authority is formal recognition of position within an organization. It can be defined within the organizational structure or hierarchy and with a job description. Because of its formal designation, a person with authority has the power to carry out directives and make decisions, but its scope is limited.

Power differs in that it cannot be easily described and can exist anywhere within the organization. True power does not need to flow only from the top down into the organization. It can therefore be formal or informal, recognized or not, legitimate or not. Individuals can derive their power from personal traits or from the locus of their position. It is well established that there are five sources of power: referent, expert, legitimate, reward, and coercive.

Those individuals who possess referent power have followers who like them. In other words, people follow these leaders because they like the person. The stability of such power is limited and uneasy, of course. If people stop liking you, you lose your power. The most stable source of power comes from expertise. A person who knows more than others in a given area has expert power and will be followed because of that expertise. Of course, legitimate power is formal and derived from a person's position of authority. While more stable than some sources of power, it is limited in scope and range. Employees follow the position, not the person.

As the name would suggest, reward power comes from the ability to reward followers for desired behavior. Rewards can be monetary or in the form of promotions and recognition. A person with reward power is bounded by the limits to the awards they can provide. Coercive power, conversely, comes from the ability to punish others by taking away position, compensation, or recognition. This source of power is even more limited than reward power.

A little side-story might be meaningful, here. This account may shed some light on how a virtuous leader differentiates between power and authority. In March 2011, the Reverend Jesse Jackson visited the University of Wisconsin Oshkosh in order to encourage young people to get out and vote. The following is a paraphrased recollection of a portion of his remarks.[4]

The Reverend began,

> Working people often tell me they have no power. But that is not true. They may not have formal authority of position on the job, but they certainly have power. They have the power of their values, and their beliefs, and their convictions. They have the power of those people with whom they surround themselves. You see, they have all the power and influence they need; they have the real power. They truly have the power to make change. You must never forget where your power comes from and where you can exert it.

Washington Post reporter Sally Jenkins wrote, "Scores of would-be overseers interpret power as something imposed on others from the top-down . . . only to find out they have lost the room and then their jobs."[5] Jenkins went on to quote Steve Kerr, the coach of the Golden State Warriors. "The source of true power is buy-in. A coach has to have the humility to ask for their input."[6]

What kind of power and authority do coaches and athletes possess? What is the best way for them to influence others? What about leaders in the education arena? Clearly, each person is a unique case. Where does the reader's influence come from? What are the subsequent strengths and concerns with their approaches?

Now it's time to circle back to the theoretical underpinnings of leadership studies. Trait theories, as the name suggests, believe leaders are born with particular traits that give them an innate ability to lead. Process theories, on the other hand, can best be described as the leader's position of authority in relation to the workers and to the responsibilities they carry out. These leaders can be taught how to lead.

Northouse describes the characteristics or traits most associated with leadership according to the literature.[7] These include the following: intelligence, self-confidence, determination, integrity, and sociability. It is hard to argue these personal attributes. Others have expanded the list to include such dispositions as charisma,[8] values,[9] and emotional intelligence.[10]

There is a great deal of academic literature devoted to understanding process approaches to leadership. In fact, hundreds of graduate school programs and businesses alike are devoted to developing the latent talents of potential leaders. This notion rests on the understanding that leaders are made, not born. Technical skills of the job, human skills in terms of working with people, and conceptual skills for working with ideas or a vision make up these attributes. Colleges focus their attention on teaching the skill sets they find most appropriate for the jobs tomorrow's leaders will need.

Much of this recent research has focused on leadership styles. Often, this work is divided into task and relationship behaviors of the leaders. A quick scan of the literature shows several leadership styles emerge in nearly every study: democratic, laissez-faire, autocratic, coaching, pacesetting, servant, transactional, and transformational[11] (figure 1.3).

Leaders who use the coaching style can best be described by their work with individual team members to identify their strengths and areas for growth to meet the organization's needs. These leaders work closely with their staff members to develop their requisite knowledge and skills. Pacesetting leaders set goals for their team and then establish the standards of accountability. They supervise, motivate, monitor, and provide feedback to their employees to the degree they reach their goals.

Autocratic leaders follow the traditional top-down approach of telling their employees what to do, how to do it, and when it's due. "They do the hiring, and they do the firing." They are your prototypical bosses. Conversely, laissez-faire leaders prefer a hands-off approach. They claim their staff are professionals and know what they are doing, so they need little direction. Speculation is that these are often out-of-touch supervisors who truly are more disinterested than trusting of their staff. In other words, it may be fair to say they are lazy bosses.

Democratic leaders actively seek employee input on various goals and tasks and then share this with senior administration who makes the final decisions together. These leaders don't seek votes or input on every task, but rather solicit feedback on strategic goals and initiatives.[12] They use democratic values and principles to guide decision-making and leverage the expertise of the professionals they employ. This model will receive special attention in the final chapters.

Servant leaders build and develop a culture of support for both the employees and for the mission of the institution. They lead by example always focusing on the vision and those responsible for it. "It was [Robert] Greenleaf's belief that leadership ought to be based on serving the needs of others and on helping those who are served to become 'healthier, wiser, freer, more autonomous, more likely themselves to become servants.'"[13]

Transactional leaders use a very traditional approach. They reward employees for meeting expectations and may be punitive in some way when employees don't meet expectations. As the name implies, the leader is continually in a state of transaction with employees to get them to meet the organization's needs. Much like autocratic leaders, transactional leaders may act more as bosses or managers than true leaders. Their modus operandi is akin to "I'll give you A if you do B."

Transformational leaders are on the opposite end of the continuum. As the name would imply, these leaders transform both the organization and those who work in it. These leaders build a culture of shared understanding and ownership in order to help both meet their individual and collective goals and aspirations. Servant leaders and transformational leaders share many of the same dispositions and visions.

In reality whether the leader prefers a certain style or model over others, it is rare to see them only relying solely on one approach. Based on context, circumstances, and need, most leaders use some form of situational leadership drawing upon techniques, styles, and approaches best suited for the time or situation. This collective approach was first described by Hersey and Blanchard.[14] The model explains leaders need to provide more or less degrees of support and direction to employees, dependent on the context at hand. Some circumstances or some people need more direction at a given moment and be given less autonomy, while at other times, the opposite approach may be more appropriate.

In a very similar fashion, Glickman created a situational supervisory continuum based on individual needs of the employee.[15] In this model, the leader shifts their degree of responsibility from or toward themselves and to or from the employee. (See figure 1.1). The relationship slides from directive to collaborative and to nondirective. Rookie employees and those needing more support would require more directional leadership, while seasoned professionals would need more nondirectional feedback from the supervisor and more professional freedom and autonomy, for example.

As can be seen in the chart, where more directional guidance is deemed necessary, the supervisor plays a greater role and takes on more responsibility compared to the employee. In cases where an employee has matured and

1	2	3	4	5	6	7	8	9	10
Listening	Clarifying	Encouraging	Reflecting	Presenting	Problem Solving	Negotiating	Directing	Standardizing	Reinforcing
E s Clusters of Behaviors		Nondirective			Collaborative				e S Directive Control

Key:
E = Maximum Employee responsibility
e = Minimum employee responsibility
S = Maximum Supervisor responsibility
s = Minimum supervisor responsibility

Figure 1.1 Supervisory Continuum. *Source*: Adapted from Carl Glickman, et al. *Supervision of Instruction: A Developmental Approach.* Boston, MA: *Allyn & Bacon.* 1998. 120-121.

is considered a very capable professional, they take on more ownership with more nondirectional support needed by the supervisor. A football coach may treat a veteran star athlete different than a newly hired free agent, or an offensive coordinator different than a young apprentice position coach.

As such, some leaders or supervisors attempt to better understand their employees, as well as to help their employees better see how they are perceived by their colleagues. In other words, they wish to help their colleagues better reflect upon themselves. These employers use the "Johari Window," to assist them.[16] The name for this model, believe it or not, was coined after two colleagues working together named Joe and Harry.

Four quadrants are depicted (please see figure 1.2) indicating what the employer sees in the behaviors of the individual, and what the individual

	Known to Supervisor	Not Known to Supervisor
Known to Self	1. Public self	3. Private self
Not Known to Self	2. Blind self	4. Unknown self

Figure 1.2 Johari Window. *Source*: Adapted from Joseph Luft, *Group Processes: An Introduction to Group Dynamics*. New York: National Press Books, 1970.

	Coercive	Authoritative	Affiliative	Democratic	Pacesetting	Coaching
Modus Operandi	Demands immediate Compliance	Mobilizes people	Creates harmony & builds emotional bonds	Forges consensus through participation	Sets high standards for performance	Develops people for the future
Style	"Do what I tell you."	"Come with me."	"People come first."	"What do you think?"	"Do as I do, now."	"Try this."
Emotional Intelligence Competency	Drive to achieve initiative, Self-control	Self-confidence empathy, change	Empathy, building relationships	Collaboration, team leadership	Conscientiousness, drive to achieve, initiative	Developing others' empathy, self-awareness
Works Best	In a crisis, Problem Employee	New vision clear direction	Heal rifts or motivate during stressful circumstances	To build consensus or get input from valuable employees	To get quick results from a highly motivated and competent team	Help an employee improve performance or develop strengths
Overall Impact	Negative	Mostly positive	Positive	Positive	Negative	Positive

Figure 1.3 Leadership Styles. *Source*: Adapted summary of leadership styles from Daniel Goleman, "Leadership that gets Results," *Harvard Business Review*, 78-90, March 2000.

knows about themselves. The quadrants (as adapted, here) are the following: the public self, the private self, the blind self, and the unknown self. It is the role of the supervisor to help the employee become aware of their blind self and the unknown self in order for them to improve where necessary.

The public self is clearly known to both the employee and to others—it is common knowledge. The private self includes things only the person knows about themselves; others are unaware. The blind self are things that others may realize about the person, but they themselves are unaware. Finally, the unknown self are those things that neither the person nor others know about them. Both supervisors and coaches certainly use versions of the Johari Window to help people self-reflect.

Much more has been written recently about particular qualities leaders exhibit.[17] These include the following: integrity, ability to delegate, communication, self-awareness, gratitude, learning agility, influence, and empathy. While a number of these abilities might be innate to some people, they can certainly be recognized and strengthened or honed.

Karl Haden and Rob Jenkins have re-imagined this "qualities" discussion by focusing on key virtues of exceptional leaders.[18] These nine classical virtues are as imperative today as they were in antiquity, according to the authors. These virtues include the following: humility, honesty, courage, perseverance, hope, charity, balance, wisdom, and justice. Practicing these virtues and helping others in the organization to achieve them, as well will better enable any institution to be successful in meeting both individual and collective goals and to reach the expectations of the organization's mission.

Are the best coaches and athletes born to lead, or are they made into leaders? What about the best leaders in our educational systems? Perhaps it is not an either/or proposition. Perhaps some leaders are born, and some are made. Perhaps people are born with certain characteristics that lend themselves to leadership potential but can be honed with practice and training. In any case, what are those attributes which best correspond to effective leaders?

No matter the preferred approach employed by the leader, their conception of the employees' motivations is critical. Douglas McGregor developed the seminal study of management with his descriptions of the binary Theory X and Theory Y to understand supervisory approaches to human motivation. Theory X managers have a more traditional belief of supervising employees, whereas Theory Y supervisors deal more in the relational realm of administration. The basic features of Theory X posit:

(1) Average workers are by nature indolent—they work as little as possible.
(2) They lack ambition, dislike responsibility, and prefer to be led.
(3) They are inherently self-centered, indifferent to organizational needs.

(4) They are by nature resistant to change.
(5) They are gullible, not very bright, ready dupes of the charlatan and demagogue.

The basic features of Theory Y posit:

(1) Management is responsible for organizing the elements of production enterprise—money, materials, equipment, and people—in the interest of economic (educational) ends.
(2) People are *not* by nature passive or resistant to organizational needs. If they appear so, it is as a result of negative experience in organizations.
(3) The motivation, potential for development, the capacity for assuming responsibility, and the readiness to direct behaviors toward organizational goals are all present in people; management does not put them there. It is a responsibility of the management to make it all possible for people to recognize and develop these human characteristics for themselves.
(4) The essential task of management is to arrange organizational conditions and methods of operation so that people can achieve their own goals *best* by directing *their* own efforts toward organizational objectives (all emphasis in original).[19]

With that all said, Theory X simply states employees are lazy and need to be supervised. Theory Y, on the other hand, sees employees as hardworking and loyal to their institutions. The former model relies on extrinsic motivation, while the latter expects administration to support intrinsic approaches. Undoubtedly, each of us can identify colleagues who are more characteristic of either Theory X or Y. Of course, most circumstances we find ourselves in fall somewhere in between.

It has been suggested that if an employee should exhibit Theory X characteristics, it is because they have been oppressed by supervisors and a system that does not embrace and support individualism, creativity, and autonomy. They have been driven down into such despair. Considering higher education relies on a highly educated and professional workforce, it would seem clear that Theory Y would best be suited for colleges. Unfortunately, Theory X beliefs and approaches are used more often than naught, even today. This is our mimetic isomorphism—it is all we know, because it is the only approach we have been taught or experienced.

An interesting rhetorical question: does the reader of this book consider themselves more of a Theory X or Theory Y person? What does the reader think about his or her colleagues? Might different leadership approaches be used for different types of workers? No matter the case, leaders should be congruent in their approaches to supervision, motivation, and organizational structure and policies with their fundamental beliefs about those people they lead. This is the focus of chapter 4—"Putting It All Together."

Finally, German sociologist Max Weber showed great concern that leadership in the hands of a single person was dangerous.[20] He had plenty of historical evidence upon which to draw with the likes of Napoleon, Hitler, and others. He felt the need to spread power out across the organization with a trained professional class—a bureaucracy. These collective individuals would be highly trained, skilled, and foremost objective. They would be beholden to the system and mission, and not to their own vanity or whims. The impact of bureaucratic models has been enormous on motivation theory and even more on how we structure our organizations, as will be described in the following chapters, respectively.

THE INTERVIEWS

So, what do we believe? Are leaders born or are they made? What characteristics do elite coaches and athletes possess? What approaches have they found to be most suitable and successful? Who have they learned the most from and what are the lessons they learned?

These are the broad types of questions which emerge from the examination of the literature just noted. From these broad topics, the following specific questions were created:

(1) Who was the best leader you learned from?
(2) What made them such an excellent role model?
(3) Without naming anyone, can you think of a poor leader and what made them so poor?
(4) Are the best leaders born or are they made?
(5) What do the best leaders do? (Answers shared in chapter 4.)
(6) Can you tell us of any great books you've read on great leaders?
(7) Describe your approach or style to leadership? (Answers shared in chapter 4.)
(8) Describe any type of leadership training you've had.
(9) What kind of power do you have?
(10) How do you measure successful leadership?
(11) Is it best to be loved or feared?

You would expect world-class athletes and coaches to share stories of famous contemporaneous leaders who shaped and molded them into the stars they became. In many instances, you would be right. In just as many cases, the people who had the most influence were parents, grandparents, as well as high school coaches and teachers.

In virtually all instances, themes quickly emerged and common characteristics or dispositions occurred time and time again. For instance, these inspirational leaders had a high degree of personal integrity, were excellent communicators, and were relationship builders. They cared about the individual and were the consummate role models. More often than not, their biggest influence came from their informal relationships; they were well organized, had an exceptional personal work ethic, and had a calming influence.

The stories of the athletes and coaches tell it the best. The informal and personal relationships between coaches and players, and between coaches and coaches, often had the greatest impact. What we see on television are the formal and structured relationships. These visible interactions are hardly the most compelling stories, though.

For example, Bart Andrus—a former assistant coach to Tennessee Titans and St. Louis Rams head football coach Jeff Fisher—told of an incident that impacted him for the rest of his life. Andrus had coached under Fisher earlier in his career and then went to NFL Europe to serve as a head coach. Later, Andrus returned to the Titans. Coach Fisher called his assistant coach into his office.

"I've placed a special clause into your contract," began Fisher. The coach braced himself for the bad news. "I am adding to your contract a stipulation that the Titans will pay for airplane tickets three weekends this season so you can return home to watch your son play his high school games. You will be back in time to coach on Sunday." As Bart Andrus left Fisher's office with tears in his eyes he turned to glance over his shoulder. Coach Fisher had tears in his eyes, too. "I would do anything for that man."

Green Bay sportscaster and former college player Burke Griffin told of a different hero—Reggie White. "He had an aura about him. When he spoke, people listened. He had a sense of humor, but he was direct and pulled no punches." Former San Francisco 49er and Green Bay Packer player and coach Harry Sydney had fond recollections of other player leaders. Joe Montana was extremely intelligent, and he carried himself in a special way. Bill Walsh was a class act in everything he did. Brett Favre and Tom Brady made everyone around them better in everything they did.

Los Angeles Dodgers baseball coach Dave Roberts was a servant leader. Ralston Cash was drafted by the Dodgers and expressed, "Everyday Coach Roberts picked up his players' lunch dishes so they could continue on with their responsibilities. He taught me about Emotional Intelligence, Grit, and Perseverance. He gave you all the time you needed." Famed knuckleball pitcher Charlie Hough helped Ralston become a student of psychology so that he could become a better pitcher and find success after athletics.

Reggie White was also mentioned by Harry Sydney. "Reggie taught me it's okay to be a physical Christian." Jeff Reinbold—former CFL head coach at Winnipeg—was an assistant coach for Dick Vermeil while at the Rams and the Chiefs. "Coach Vermeil was extremely organized and always empathetic. He never demeaned anyone; he always focused on the human side." Brigham Young University head football coach, LaVell Edwards, gained special praise from then graduate assistant Bart Andrus. "What impressed me the most about LaVell was the way he managed his coaches and talked to his players—casually, and how he led a group of young men."

National doubles tennis champion and International Women's Tennis Hall of Famer Dr. Ann Lebedeff credited "the women who pioneered women's tennis—" Dr. Joan Johnson, Billie Jean King, and Dr. Ann Pittman. "These women served as my mentors from the very beginning. They showed me what it took to be successful. Billie Jean King, for example, taught me the mindset and psychology of being a strong woman."

NFL wide receiver Tavarres King played collegiately at the University of Georgia. Tavarres spoke of Coach Mark Richt with high regard. "He walked his talk; everything was real, his lifestyle, the way he treated people. He made us better men." King played with Peyton Manning for the Denver Broncos.

> Peyton demanded a lot of himself and others. We respected him. He was a player/coach. He excelled and made us think as individuals about what we were doing. He was the sheriff, and he knew what it took to win and what it took to be a professional.

NFL defensive tackle for the Pittsburg Steelers and Cleveland Brown Darryl Sims said another former NFL star mentored him when he was a young Wisconsin Badger.

> Arnold Jeter recruited me. He had an innate ability to motivate young student-athletes, and he directly impacted my success. Arnold taught me how to prepare, how to study, and how to compete. He was not pretentious, but he could be stern and get me back on track when I needed it.

Juwan Green has played wide receiver for the Atlanta Falcons and Detroit Lions. Juwan noted that his AAU basketball coach was assertive but excelled at getting the entire team to excel at a particular level—the team would only be as strong as its weakest player. On the other hand, his unit coach on the Falcons, Raheem Morris, was a humble man who always gave his honest opinion; he built relationships with all the players as individuals.

Milwaukee Bucks scout and former women's college basketball coach at Western Michigan University Ron Stewart made special mention of Lon Kruger.

I was an assistant coach when he was head coach at the University of Florida. He was an outstanding coach, both in the game and day-to-day. He was even keeled, not too high and not too low. What impressed me the most was the way he treated people, and how he coached people. He honored others. He was a program builder. University of Indiana coach Bobby Knight taught me a great deal about discipline. Bob Hammond (former Bucks General Manager) was a true friend and associate and did a great deal to help my career.

Some of the best leaders came from the Military. A former assistant football coach at Yale and an active USA Boxing coach, Gordon Marino, recalls this advice from his mentor Colonel Gordon Calkins. Marino worked under Colonel Calkins guiding the boxing team at Virginia Military Institute. Marino recalls this advice from his mentor, "You have to have an ego to be a good coach but you have to keep an eye on it and remember it's not about you, it's about the athletes you are coaching."

West Point baseball star Jon Reinebold later served on Special Ops in Qatar during the Iraq War and was a battalion commander in Japan. Jon expressed admiration for Military Commander Gary Harrell. "He taught me through his actions—how to react in pressure situations. He was calm, rational, took in information from around him, all under stress, and made sound decisions." Olympic team handball star Jennifer Demby said her father was a former soldier and a boxer. Both he and her mother instilled in her a state of confidence with continued encouragement.

John Roberts is head rugby coach at the University of South Carolina. His grandfather was a Marine and raised him. "He led by example, had a tremendous work ethic, was consistent, predictable, a rock." Retired head football coach at the University of Wisconsin Oshkosh, Pat Cerroni, was himself a member of the Air Force. He learned work ethic, discipline, and organization during his years of service.

Many times, it is those homegrown heroes who make the biggest impact. These are the unheralded or lesser-known high school and college coaches that players will remember for the rest of their lives. Former U.S. Olympian and Wimbledon star Dick Stockton spoke of his college coach at Trinity University, Clarence Mabry. "He was a father-figure and role model. He was unique. He knew what to say to everyone as an individual—not the same message to everyone. Clarence would talk with you in private. He had an impact on my entire life."

Attributes and dispositions most often associated with these high school and college coaches include the following qualities: caring, role models, motivators, organized, intelligent, and adaptable. They are by their very nature, and explicitly stated, teachers. Former football player at Northern Michigan University and the University of Wisconsin Oshkosh Fred Roethlisberger described UW Oshkosh strength and conditioning coach Steve Brown as one who gave high challenge and high support and was a great communicator. Roethlisberger also noted that his head coach Pat Cerroni was entrepreneurial and adaptable.

Another one of Cerroni's players is now Sol Ross University head football coach Barry Derickson. Derickson said of his former coach,

> Pat Cerroni adapted over time. He was charismatic and expected all players to take their own motivation and self-direction in order to grow as leaders. He transformed himself. Players created their own legacies and took leadership development seriously. He was transparent and honest to recruits and their families.

Who did Cerroni find most inspirational? "Coach Guerin. He was awesome in the classroom. He could get anything out of anybody. I modeled myself after him. He influenced me to be a teacher." Charlie Birdsong served as the high school volleyball and softball coach for college rugby player Abbey Dondanville. "He was always looking for ways to make us better, not only athletes, but better people. For example, sometimes he would cancel practice and have us go to read to elementary children. He always modeled giving back to the community."

Piedmont University's head women's basketball coach Jamie Purdy was grateful for her high school coach Paul Webb who served as a role model at a critical time of her life. "He was a family-man of high morals and values. He was like a father-figure to me." University of Texas softball player, Gabby Smith Roethlisberger, expressed similar praise for her high school coach. "Coach Tuffly showed he cared. He built relationships with the players and their families. He was thoughtful toward everyone on the team."

Former University of Maryland football standout Dean Green highlighted his high school assistant principal Dr. Perry. "He was my father-figure and mentor. He set the tone and gave us direction for our lives after we graduated school. For him, the students always came first." Similarly, former LaGrange wide receiver Marcus Campbell shared that his high school coach, Leroy Ryals "meant business. He taught us real-life experience—bigger than football. He inspired us to be a better player on the field and a better person off the field. He saw our potential."

There are just as many stories about heroic parents and grandparents; these are the stories which warm our hearts. One NFL player, Tavarres King, recalled, "The way my parents went about their business, how they handled themselves in hard times and dedicated themselves to others—that's what I remember." Duke University football star Joshua Pickett said his parents were the support system that helped him as he transitioned to college.

Another NFL player, Evan Oglesby, fondly told of his grandmother. "She put her life on hold and provided for others. She was always helping people, and people respected her." A Hall of Fame Women's volleyball player, Nicky Bowman, told of a Native American village elder: "She showed me how to represent and of my responsibility to my community and future generations."

Unwavering and steadfast dedication and caring spirits characterize these parents and grandparents. Other attributes and dispositions most often cited are selfless, work ethic, role models, and standard-bearers. Again, speaking of his grandfather, John Roberts recalled, "My grandfather led a quiet purposeful life and led by example. He woke up at 4:30 every morning and was a manual laborer. He was always there for you. As humans, we crave predictability."

Olympic cyclist and many times national champion Jame Carney was unequivocal in his admiration for his father.

> My father gave me opportunities and allowed me to choose for myself. He was always honest with me and expected the same in return. He instilled standards in me and taught me how to set my own standards and sense of accountability. My father taught me cause-and-effect by showing how hard work has pay-back in success.

Another Olympian, and president of the Atlanta Braves Foundation, speedskater Mike Plant was effusive in praising his parents.

> My dad taught me about integrity and to take personal responsibility, sometimes with tough love, to always be honest, and to have a personal standard of excellence in all that you do. By his actions he showed me resiliency and perseverance, and how to collaborate with others. Both my parents had incredible work ethics. My mom was an incredible organizer and the foundation of our family.

These elite coaches and athletes were just as quick to point out stories of leaders who did not earn their admiration, nor would serve as healthy role models. These antagonists share some common features, as well. Often, they are egotistical, and all effort is in creating and maintaining their image. They are quick to take credit and to dish out blame. Their behavior edges toward unethical and at times may be abusive or manipulative. Many are unorganized and have not earned the respect of their colleagues or players.

When you are leading professionals and highly motivated individuals, "it's about building relationships," according to former head football coach at the University of Wisconsin River Falls John O'Grady. "The bad coaches don't build relationships." NFL star Tavarres King continued, "In the NFL, you are a leader of men—treat them with respect. The worst leaders are about themselves. They don't respect others as men. They take their positions with too much power and are personally-driven rather than team-driven."

Former U.S. Women's Olympic medalist in cycling, Sarah Hammer noted, "coaches who ruled with fear—they manipulated situations and their athletes. They were emotionally abusive, and at times the worst thing they would do was ignore you." Piedmont University Athletic Director and former baseball coach Jim Peeples expressed examples of "people with very low self-esteem but act arrogant. You aren't allowed to question their authority. They don't take the time to get to know you."

Chan Gailey, former NFL head coach for the Dallas Cowboys and the Buffalo Bills talked of a previous coach. "I learned a lot from him—how not to treat people. He was degrading, belittling, and talked down to people in front of others." Middle Tennessee State University defensive lineman Mike Owensby related a story of a former coach. "He did nothing but tear you down, was never positive." Former college football and lacrosse player Mike Hartman noted these poor leaders are divisive and create cliques. Abbey Dondanville agreed. "The poor leaders punish and embarrass, divide people, create cliques and silos."

Coach Marino, who is also a veteran philosophy professor at St. Olaf, observed "There are lots of bad ones in academia as well—that is, bureaucrats who don't care enough to listen to others and establish the relationships that will bring the best out of people."

In a similar vein, Darryl Sims recalled a couple of negative examples from his collegiate years.

> They did not have the pulse of the kids—didn't know the kids. They weren't personable and had not established the relationships; it showed on game days. The players didn't believe in those coaches—the players started to look out for themselves and their own stats—not for the team.

Jennifer Demby expressed, "Coaches who are yellers or embarrass their athletes—they simply aren't effective."

Marcus Campbell stipulated:

> They have no leadership skills; they're like dictators, always pointing fingers at others when times get tough. The best coaches don't show favoritism. They

help you fit in with a team-work approach, they are excellent communicators, and they build mutual trust.

Juwan Green added, "Coaches who don't listen to their players and are stuck in their old ways will never get the best out of their players."

Gretchen Rush, professional women's tennis player and university coach and professor, also castigated some leaders in higher education. "The problem with academic jobs is there are too many rules and not enough freedom or ability to be creative as professionals. There needs to be a balance between autonomy and accountability."

Former NFL Europe coach Larry Owens did not respect leaders who were too "militaristic. They treated everyone and every situation the same. There was no response to the circumstances. People didn't respect that." John Roberts added, "They make it difficult to follow; they have no integrity. The bad ones make it all about themselves; they don't focus on the human values." Former CFL head coach for the Hamilton Tiger-Cats Marcel Bellefeuille noted concerns about leaders who have no vision which then causes the team to struggle and perish. Similarly, those who are transactional in their interactions with their assistants and players fail to earn the requisite respect.

Moreover, Jame Carney expressed concerns about people who were "the over aggressive, hyper managers. Every athlete's needs are different, so a cookie-cutter approach doesn't work. And you need to check your ego." University of Texas softball star Gabby Smith Roethlisberger agreed. "Your ego is the most expensive thing you own." Joshua Pickett added, "Poor leaders are the ones who you trust, but let you down under difficult circumstances—their true character shows then."

With examples of exemplary leaders and those we hope to never become, the next question becomes: "Are the best leaders born or are they made?" While the responses were wide-ranging, not one coach or athlete expressed that the best leaders are purely born leaders. Every interviewee stated these leaders are either made over time through experience and training, or they may be born with some natural tendencies toward leadership, but these attributes are honed over the years. Sometimes leadership emerges in the context of necessity in a given time or circumstance.

To be blunt, Jon Reinebold argued, "Learned behavior. 100%! All leaders fail. They need to be taught how to lead and be successful, to learn from their failures." Larry Owens shared that leaders need to be developed. He learned by observing and in turn he developed confidence. Jame Carney said that "the kids need to see no work is beneath you." Chan Gailey added, "These leaders have made it to the American dream, because they earned it; they are self-made."

Marcel Bellefeuille, head coach of Ottawa University, agreed.

The best leaders develop leadership skills; you lead by the example you set. They are good teachers. It's truly all about process, about being pragmatic, and about being able to structure the culture and the work of members of the organization to work together to enact your goal and vision.

Bart Andrus said leaders are both born and made. "They have to have a willingness to take on the mantle, but they develop their skills—to rise up and learn." Ann Lebedeff noted, "Leaders are made by their circumstances of their life and the context. They have to learn lessons that they are taught." Abbey Dondanville concurred. "They are made by experience and by learning from watching others. There might be some innate characteristics, but they are enhanced by learning."

Mike Owensby felt leadership is both innate and learned. "They may be born with the 'It Factor,' but to be good it has to be learned. Like a natural athlete needs to be honed." Harry Sydney also talked of the "It Factor." They're born with it and then they learn the skills to magnify it. It's also context-based—they step up to whatever situation they're in. Willie Garrett, former college football player concurred. "You might be born with talent, but leadership is about how you use your talent."

Are these elite athletes and coaches avid readers? Do they have formal education to become leaders? A good many have read extensively and have had special training. Many coaches require their players to read particular books, be they on leadership, inspirational, or motivational.

While the list of their readings is expansive, the authors most often cited by these elite coaches and athletes include books by John Wooden and Sun Tzu. Books about or by Vince Lombardi top the list, as well. John Wooden was mentioned the most often, by far.

Many of our coaches have taught courses at the college level and many came from the ranks of high school teachers. John O'Grady, Ann Lebedeff, Gretchen Rush, and Gordon Marino always maintained a significant teaching load during or after coaching. Chan Gailey taught a leadership course to all freshmen football players at Georgia Tech.

Nicky Bowman, Ann Lebedeff, Abbey Dondanville, and Gordon Marino all have doctorate degrees. Many others have master's degrees in Educational Leadership. Mike Owensby was a Woodrow Wilson Scholar. Jon Reinebold's entire experience at West Point emphasized leadership. Both Jim Peeples and Darryl Sims noted special seminars and workshops hosted by the NCAA as beneficial for advancing collegiate leaders in athletics. All of the coaches with NFL experience have benefitted be internships, graduate assistantships, and/or camps.

Clearly, coaches have formal authority, but what kind of power do they have? The answers might be surprising. Other than deciding who makes the team and who plays, what kind of power do coaches have? The answer is "very little," according to Larry Owens.

> The kids have the power; they're the ones who are getting it done on the field. They have the power to decide their effort, how much time they will give in the weight room and film study, and ultimately determine how successful they will be.

Ann Lebedeff explained that power originates from your reputation and character. "Especially for a female coach, once you have established a positive and respected reputation in coaching, your team will listen." Jennifer Demby agreed. "Your power comes from the respect your opponents show you." Jon Reinebold extended this line of reasoning. "I certainly have positional authority, but if you rely on that, you won't get very far. You have to relate to the people. Otherwise, you get resentment."

In many respects, it comes down not to power but to influence. Dick Stockton noted, "You help them understand they're building a resume. They learn good habits of time management, being punctual, being a good teammate, being in control of your emotions—being a good citizen."

Mike Owensby expressed it in terms of empowering others. "You give them and show them opportunities which can lead to their success. Then, you surround them with support." Gretchen Rush was emphatic, "The best coaches empower their athletes and give them time to grow." Joshua Pickett concurred, "As you learn and grow from the lessons the coach teaches you, you become more empowered. They empower you to make decisions on the field, during the games."

John Roberts smiled when he said, "Power over others is an illusion." Echoing Roberts, Marcel Bellefeuille stated, "Power and control are an illusion. It's about creating a culture." In fact, Tavarres King stipulated, "In the NFL I learned that I only have power over myself through my attitude and my own work ethic."

When pressed to describe how successful leadership should be measured, these elite coaches and athletes did not disappoint. As a matter of fact, their responses were affirming and congruent with everything that has been said to this point. In other words, their words were consistent throughout. For example, Mike Hartman impressed: "It's not so much on the wins/losses, but did the guys get better, learn from their mistakes? Did they come together as a team?"

Without fail, the human dimension, growth of the individual or the team, was the driving measure of success to these coaches and players. "Success is measured by seeing the development of players and young men, not about the wins and losses," according to Larry Owens. Mike Owensby explained,

> At DI, the university looks at wins and losses. But the coaches look at success as the development of the players. However, you can't develop the players if you don't get enough wins—you won't be around long enough to make that impact.

Hall of Famer Gretchen Rush explained, "Wins and losses are important, but it comes down to personal growth. What drives winning? It's your values and your experiences. The winning takes care of itself after the personal growth." Another Hall of Famer, Ann Lebedeff had a slightly different take. "Success never involves the word, 'winning.' Winning is temporary. Success is about meeting the next challenge—the challenge of the day. It's ultimately about people's development, about courage, and about unselfishness."

Marcel Bellefeuille uses the Greek word, "Arete," which is defined as excellence in all its forms. "You bring something to its most excellent form, build it to excellence from its potential. I always want to invest in others' futures and leave any organization better than when I got there." "Success is measured by the result, by the effort. Did I leave it all out there? Did I learn lessons and not make the same mistakes? Leaders need to adapt to the situation, not make the situation adapt to them," according to Olympian Jame Carney.

Fellow Olympian Sarah Hammer expressed success comes about "by bringing out the best in the athletes and staff—to do the best they can under their circumstances." Barry Derickson added, "You measure success by being a positive influence in their lives, by helping them take personal charge of their lives." Gabby Smith Roethlisberger concluded that success is measured "by the impact you have on people, to help them change and grow." Fred Roethlisberger agreed. "It's about growth of players as individuals and as a team. Did they change on *and* off the field? Did the team improve?"

Expanding on the concept of team, former boxing coach and college football coach Gordon Marino explained, "You work to build a strong group identity; build team-identity and get the players to bond and stick together, all while learning self-discipline." John O'Grady continued, "There is the obvious wins and losses, but you measure the coach by who he surrounds himself with, and did he create a cohesive group that worked together toward a common goal?"

University of South Carolina coach John Roberts said,

> When I interviewed for the job I talked about the journey of growing, meeting challenges and milestones. You develop a culture of accountability to yourself

and to your teammates. That's the qualitative. There is, of course, the quantitative of wins and losses.

Jennifer Demby explained, "You know from the feedback you get. Are you able to learn lessons and find the positive? It's often the intangibles."
From a collegiate athlete's perspective, Joshua Pickett explained,

> You get buy-in from the players. You earn the players' respect and bring the team together for a shared understanding of the mission and vision. Winning follows from that. You need to build culture and empower the players to build that culture.

Former DI football player Dean Green explained that coaches earn respect by their successes. People gravitate toward successful leaders.
DIII Athletic Director Darryl Sims started with Wins and Losses.

> You need to measure the wins and losses for sure. The coaches need to win 60% of their games or more. I measure them on who they recruit—kids who can handle the rigors of college life—academics, emotional, physical—are they ready? How they interact with and get involved with the campus and the community.

Marcus Campbell explained, "Excellent leaders lead with their morals and values. Their aim is to uplift their men to better their lives. It is about personal connections."
Do the thoughts of professional coaches and athletes mesh with those of the Olympians and collegiates? Chan Gailey stated,

> Are you in it to get measured—to get a pat on the back? Do what you think is right. For the pros its first about wins and losses and then about making a difference in people's lives. You can't do the latter without success at the former.

Jeff Reinebold agreed, "At the pro-level it's greatly about wins and losses—that's cut and dried. But we have to prepare them for what's after football." His brother, Jon Reinebold, added,

> At the highest levels it has to go with wins and losses to some degree of course, but it's really about the development of the person, the athlete. John Wooden was great. He talked of the satisfaction in knowing that a player knew he did his best.

Coach Bart Andrus explained,

> In the pros it's going to be about wins and losses, of course, but you want to be able to do it in a way that is comfortable to you with respect to your values and integrity, and where people can enjoy it.

Similarly, Harry Sydney said, "It's based on how others grow. In football, ultimate success is also shown by a super bowl ring."

Tavarres King expressed a professional player's perspective.

> In the NFL it's of course about wins and losses. Everybody in the organization needs to be about wins. But the best leaders also get a group of different individuals to have one goal and work together as one. It's about developing a culture. Coach Fox at Denver was the best at developing that culture.

Ron Stewart posited,

> Leaders need to be able to change with the times. It's about taking care of the players and their families. The Milwaukee Bucks are great at this. It's not all about the wins; you need the wins, though, so you can do the rest.

The Atlanta Braves' Mike Plant concluded, "You don't measure success with just data. While that's important, it's a balance along with the human element, and Atlanta excels at that."

One final leadership query was asked of these women and men. Machiavelli posed the question, "Is it better to be feared or loved?" to the new prince. Our coaches and athletes clearly disagreed with Machiavelli. As a matter of emphasis Gabby Smith Roethlisberger noted, "Fear is only for ego-maniacs! They don't build relationships." When these elite coaches and athletes did use the term "fear," however, it was in a different context.

Larry Owens was fearful that he would let his parents down; they had worked so hard for him. Jame Carney explained, "You want to be loved by your teammates, but feared by your competitors." Even Oglesby agreed, "You want your opponent to fear you on the field. In the locker room you have the fear that you will let your coach or teammates down." Kierkegaard scholar Gordon Marino turned the question upside down. "It's a false dichotomy—they go together. You always want to be loved, but I had the fear, for example, of disapproval or to let down my dad."

Jon Reinebold expressed, "People will do anything for someone they love. In the military they will put their lives on the line for the ones they love." Jeff Reinebold spoke of both love and fear. "You want to love the people who care about you. Sometimes loving someone means to hold them accountable. Fear is so short-term." He would tell his players, "All I can guarantee you is that we will face adversity together."

Bart Andrus followed,

> To be loved is better. But you also want them to be good people and good at what they do, so sometimes you have to correct them or discipline out of love

for them. Fear does not lead to long-term success. And I want our work to be pleasant.

Agreeing, Sarah Hammer noted, "Fear is only temporary and won't work for long." According to Marcus Campbell, "Fear only breeds resentment." NFL wide receiver Juwan Green provided an interesting insight. When a player is fearful of talking to a coach, then they hesitate to ask questions. They lose out on an opportunity to improve because of the fear.

Ralston Cash added, "Loved—fear is rude and is only to help the coach. Love is for we the team." Nicky Bowman was poignant in her response. "I don't want anyone to be afraid. I want us to take care of our community." When she was an athlete Jennifer Demby wanted her opponents to fear her, but as a coach for blind athletes she hopes to have a loving relationship.

Circling back to Marino's claim that fear and love is a false dichotomy, several of our coaches and athletes looked at the question through a different lens. Dick Stockton recalled competing against the Australian tennis players who were the best in the world at the time. "We competed heavily against one another, but we loved each other off the court. I would use the term, 'respect.' We respected but did not fear them. As a coach, I don't want my kids to fear me," he concluded. Joshua Pickett expressed it differently, "Fear is only good if it makes you better. Fear sometimes motivated me. I was afraid to be embarrassed, afraid of the authority figure."

Mike Owensby noted as both an athlete and coach, "It's better to be respected, but ultimately loved." Ann Lebedeff was emphatic in her response, "Loved, but respected. . . . You care about them, love them, and have their best interests at heart." Harry Sydney viewed it as respect, too. "When they want to be around you, you can have an impact on them. If they fear you, they will want to take you out and won't learn from you."

"Loved, but most important is respected and trusted. Love comes from there," according to Jeff Reinebold. Jamie Purdy agreed, "A little bit of both for respect. They need to know you love and trust them and they you, but they need to know you will hold them accountable." Abbey Dondanville explained it this way, "We loved Coach Birdsong. He elicited so much respect from us. We didn't want to disappoint him."

Love, respect, relationships, trust, support, and organized are the hallmark qualities of our best leaders. These servant leaders have the work ethic, integrity, and compassion for those around them. They help develop those in their charge to become better at their craft and as human beings. A great deal of this comes from the focus of our next chapter—how they view motivation.

NOTES

1. Niccolo Machiavelli, Translated by Ninian Hill Thomson. SDE Classics Philosophy Collection. *The Prince*. Chapter VVII (2019).

In his effort to curry favor, and its corresponding power and influence, Machiavelli wrote an essay advising the new prince lessons learned from history's leaders. Here, he suggested that it is best to be both loved and feared by your followers, but if you can only be one, it is best to be feared as it is the most stable.

2. Peter G. Northouse, *Leadership: Theory and Practice*, 5th edition (Los Angeles, CA: Sage, 2010), 4–10.

Northouse provides an erudite description and scan covering the breadth of leadership research in the field.

3. John Kotter, *What Leaders Really Do* (Cambridge, MA: Harvard Business School Press, 1999).

4. Jesse Jackson, Paraphrased speech to students at the University of Wisconsin Oshkosh—paraphrased by Perry R. Rettig (March 28, 2011).

5. Sally Jenkins, "Keys to Good Coaching," article in the *Washington Post*. Carried in the (*Atlanta Journal-Constitution*, December 26, 2021), 42.

6. Jenkins, "Keys to Good Coaching," 42.

7. Northouse, *Leadership: Theory and Practice*, 19.

8. Garry Wills, *Certain Trumpets: The Nature of Leadership* (New York: Simon & Schuster, 1995).

Here, Wills describes charismatic leadership in its original nuanced definition as proposed by Max Weber. As such, a charismatic leader is the founding leader of a concept or movement.

9. Thomas Sergiovanni, *Value-Added Leadership: How to get Extraordinary Performance in Schools* (New York: Harcourt, Brace, Jovanovich Publishers, 1990).

10. Daniel Goleman, *Emotional Intelligence: Why it can Matter More than IQ* (New York: Random House Publishing Group, 2005).

11. "What are the 7 Types of Leadership Styles?" https://www.mvorganizing.org/what-are-the-7-types-of-leadership-styles/

This is an excellent website, perhaps the most comprehensive, describing leadership styles, and leadership qualities.

"Leadership Styles: Learn the 7 Different Management Styles," https://leaders.com/articles/leadership/leadership-styles

"Five Types of Leadership Styles in Management," https://emplify.com/blog/5-types-of-leadership-styles-in-management/

"Ten Common Leadership Styles." Indeed Editorial Team. June 30, 2021. https://www.indeed.com/career-advice/career-development/10-common-leadership-styles.

"Ten Different Types of Leadership Styles," https://online.norwich.edu/academic-programs/resources/10-different-types-leadership-styles.

Below is an adapted summary of leadership styles from Daniel Goleman, "Leadership that gets Results," *Harvard Business Review* (March 2000), 78–90.

12. Perry Rettig, This democratic conceptual model will be much more thoroughly described in the final chapter of this book. This model is described for the first time in *Battles in the Trenches*.

13. Larry Spears, In the Preface xix-xx to Robert K. Greenleaf's, *The Power of Servant Leadership*. Edited by Larry C. Spears (San Francisco, CA: Berrett-Koehler Publishers, Inc. 1998).

14. Paul Hersey and Kenneth Blanchard, *Management and Organizational Behavior: Utilizing Human Resources* (Englewood Cliffs, NJ: Prentice Hall, 1969).

An excellent and erudite depiction of the model is described in Northouse, Leadership: Theory and Practice, 89–90.

15. Carl Glickman, Stephen Gordon, and Jovita Ross-Gordon, *Supervision of Instruction: A Developmental Approach* (Boston, MA: Allyn & Bacon, 1998), 119–122.

These authors go into greater detail about supervisory behavior along the continuum. Even veteran professionals might need more directional supervision if they must learn a new technology, a new system, or are failing to live up to standards, for example.

16. Joseph Luft, *Group Processes: An Introduction to Group Dynamics* (New York: National Press Books, 1970).

The "Johari Window" has been named after Joseph Luft and Harry Ingham in 1955.

17. https://www.mvorganizing.org/what-are-the-7-types-of-leadership-styles/

18. Karl Haden and Rob Jenkins, *The 9 Virtues of Exceptional Leaders: Unlocking Your Leadership Potential* (Atlanta, GA: Deeds Publishing, 2015).

This book is a tremendous read examining leadership from an entirely unique perspective. Haden wrote the forward to *Trenches*.

19. Thomas Sergiovanni and Robert Starratt, *Supervision: A Redefinition* (New York: McGraw-Hill, 1993), 15–16.

20. Robert Owens, *Organizational Behavior in Education: Adaptive Leadership and School Reform* (Boston: Pearson, Allyn & Bacon, 2004), 85.

Chapter 2

Motivation at the Highest Level

The beatings will continue until morale improves. –The boss

So much has been written about motivation. Intrinsic versus extrinsic—what approach is best? What is the role of the leader? What is the responsibility of the employee? How do the best college and pro coaches and athletes approach motivation? This chapter begins with a scan of the literature before jumping right into the interviews to find the answers to these probing questions.

Before jumping feet-first into the literature of motivation theory, however, it would be prudent for us to re-examine our own notions of our colleagues as people and as professionals or workers. In other words, what are the assumptions we make about our employees and colleagues, and subsequently how do we organize our places of work? Are our organizations structured for professionals, or more for bureaucrats, or for automatons? Is there a difference? An interesting side question: How are we ourselves best motivated? This will be a fitting place to begin our review of the literature.

THE LITERATURE

What do we believe about our own motives? What about the motives of those whom we employ? In chapter 1, we discussed the seminal work of Douglas McGregor in his binary model of Theory X and Theory Y to help us understand human motivation.[1] We learned Theory X leaders have a more traditional belief about workers and how administrators must interact with and are responsible to motivate them. Theory Y leaders, on the other hand, have a more contemporary humanistic and relational belief and approach to working with people.

Theory X workers are seen as lazy, quite frankly. They'll try to get away with doing as little work as possible. If they were self-motivated, they would have advanced to the top or further in the organization's hierarchy. They are self-centered, are not necessarily bright, and do not like change. But, because they lack ambition and drive, they are where they belong in the organization. Since they are not professionals, they need directive and corrective supervision. The bottom line—they need to be motivated by their superiors.

Theory Y employees, however, exhibit behaviors quite to the contrary. The bosses have the responsibility not to motivate, but rather to put the necessary systems in place for the workers to accomplish their responsibilities. The employees don't need external motivation, rather they are self-motivated because they are driven, have goals and ambition, and have pride in their work. They are loyal to the institution, are intelligent, are creative, and are hard-working. They like to be a part of the change process—to have a say in the direction of the organization and of their work. They seek out responsibility and support one another. As they are professionals, they are self-motivated.

A significant concern with external approaches, a Theory X view to motivation, is that employees will spend their focus on getting rewarded and not focus on the mission. Further, they will focus on avoiding punishment and needing to do just enough to get by. This is a view that creates lethargy, legalism, and minimal achievement. These are the workers in *jobs*, not *vocations*.

Even more important, when the leader takes on responsibility for motivation of others, they take ownership, and the employee abdicates responsibility. If the "superior" is responsible, then the employee can simply say, "I'm just doing what I'm told" or "It's not my fault." They have no ownership and therefore no responsibility. In as much, they are less engaged. Freedom to be responsible for one's own motivation is a two-sided coin—with the other side being professional responsibility and accountability.

As noted in chapter 1, should an employee exhibit Theory X characteristics, it is because they have been oppressed by supervisors and a system that does not embrace and support individualism, creativity, professionalism, and autonomy. Quite frankly, such feelings are the result of the employer or boss owning the responsibility of motivation. Employees, in such circumstances, are not responsible for their own motivation. Motivation happens to them and often in a form of manipulation.

Ultimately then, our beliefs or assumptions about people will likely determine how we view their motivation. If we believe people are lazy and indolent by nature, then we will use a Theory X or external approaches to motivate them; these leaders are Machiavellian in style. This is a very traditional top-down management model.

Managers might use "hard" Theory X approaches with very directive carrot and stick techniques or "soft" Theory X approaches that are more manipulative and coercive. Soft approaches focus more on making employees "feel" they are empowered or by limiting areas of their empowerment, for example. In other words, the bosses give the *perception* of democratic decision-making, yet they still "need to hold employees accountable," because they don't trust them to hold themselves to account.[2] Ultimately, motivation still remains the responsibility of the boss.

Theory Y leaders, conversely, create an environment and culture of true empowerment. They embrace professionalism and both encourage and support employee decision-making. These leaders look for opportunities for intrinsic motivation to occur. They look for diversity of opinion and always strive to coalesce around mission, vision, and shared values. They embrace open and honest dialogue with multidirectional communication and cross-functional participation. They believe in the concept of a team approach. Such leaders are not transactional in process; rather, their approach is transformational. Employees hold themselves to account. Theory Y leaders build relationships, listen, and support their professional colleagues.

We often have a view that our elite coaches and athletes are highly motivated for both themselves and for their teams. Is that true? Do these highly trained and successful people follow a more Theory X or a Theory Y approach to employee motivation? What do the readers of this book feel about people and how they should be motivated? Are their own practices congruent with the philosophies they embrace?

Another fundamental way to understand our organizations is the degree to which they are structured in a more or less professional or bureaucratic fashion. Max Weber categorized organizations into four primary groups based upon the degree to which they characterize professional and bureaucratic attributes (see figure 2.1).[3] While this professional-bureaucratic organizational structure discussion lends itself to chapter 3 of this book, its genesis derives particularly from our notions of what we believe about people and how they are motivated.

Organizations that have a high level of professional norms and standards and have a high degree of bureaucratic structures are considered "Weberian." Clearly, today's typical universities and K-12 schools fall into this category and are the model to which most organizations actually aspire. These education institutions hire highly professionalized workers yet have a highly structured bureaucracy. Hospitals would also fit this model, of course. Professionals are spread throughout the entire organization. A mix of intrinsic and extrinsic motivation is employed.

Conversely, some institutions have high levels of bureaucracy, yet few professional attributes. Much of the industrial world falls into this category. These organizations are considered "bureaucratic," as would be expected. The only professionals reside at the top of the system. A very extrinsic model of motivation is employed in order to hold the workers accountable for their work.

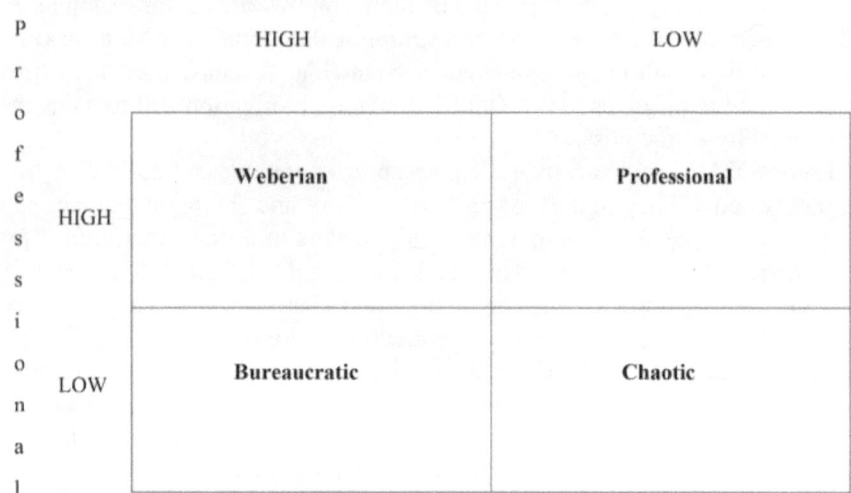

Figure 2.1   Professional-Bureaucratic Matrix.

Other institutions have high levels of professionalism with little bureaucratic regulation and oversight. These typically are small institutions originated by professional entrepreneurs. Charter schools often begin this way. However, as they become more and more successful, they grow. In order to maintain control of the values and vision of the organization, the leaders put bureaucratic structures and employees into place, with a resulting Weberian lean. Such institutions with a high degree of professional attributes are naturally considered "professional." Intrinsic motivation principles are the norm in professional organizations.

Still other institutions have low levels of professional expertise accompanied by low degrees of bureaucratic structure; they are considered "chaotic." Numerous start-up attempts are made and ultimately fail with no special expertise or standard structures as guideposts. No one wants to work in these organizations which flounder about adrift searching for some semblance of order. Without either a professional or a bureaucratic leadership model in place, these places perish. Indeed, it is the Weberian model to which most organizations ultimately gravitate.

Are our athletic organizations more professional or more bureaucratic in nature? Are they more a combination of both and in truth more Weberian? Most likely the readers of this book work in Weberian institutions and can notice similar attributes across systems.

Henry Mintzberg pressed forward with this construct of our systems behaving as professional bureaucracies (see figure 2.2).[4] In this case, the professional

Figure 2.2 Mintzberg's Professional Bureaucracy.

bureaucracy relies on the *authority of expertise*. Consequently, the professional has a significant amount of power within the organization. Professional leadership, thus, is not powerless. In fact, a key characteristic in a professional bureaucracy is complexity and uncertainty and considerable power is to be found between those dynamics. This discussion will be covered more directly in the following chapter. For now, it is worthwhile for the leader to acknowledge the degree to which their organization relies on professional staff.

No one who has graduated college with a professional degree in education could leave without becoming immersed in Abraham Maslow's Needs Hierarchy.[5] The original hierarchy is captured in figure 2.3.

Figure 2.3 Maslow's Needs Hierarchy.

Maslow's pyramid model contends that individual people are motivated by an ever-increasing hierarchy of needs. Starting at the bottom of the pyramid, people are motivated to take care of their most basic physiological needs, for example, food and water. Once these needs are sufficiently met, the next level people seek is their own safety and financial security. Once these needs have been met, the next level is a sense of love, belonging, and acceptance by others.

Once these lower-level needs are met, people are motivated by esteem and then ultimately self-actualization. The former is a sense of self-esteem and recognition by peers. The final level includes a sense of becoming whole, having personal autonomy, and self-direction. As the model suggests, each of us strives to move higher up the pyramid.

We can, however, slip back down at any time. For example, should a person's house burn down, they could slip from esteem needs to physiological needs. Similarly, a highly self-motivated professional might be given very unique and demanding new job responsibilities and subsequently slip down the hierarchy in the short term until they regain confidence and expertise.

A number of other authors have extended Maslow's Needs Hierarchy from the personal to the professional world. Lyman Porter redefined the levels[6] (see figure 2.4):

In security, workers look for pay needs, as well as seniority, retirement benefits, due process, and other fairness doctrines. If these basic needs are met, the employees are motivated by belonging, or affiliation, to both informal and formal work groups, professional associations, and the like. At the self-esteem level, workers are looking for titles, formal recognition, promotions, and other status symbols.

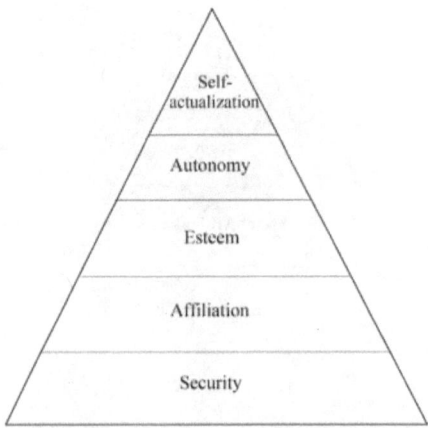

Figure 2.4 Porter's Work Needs Hierarchy.

When it comes to autonomy needs, employees want to be part of formal decision-making and have the ability to influence others and the organization. They wish to have flexibility to make their own decisions. Finally, the top level of motivation is met when employees meet their own goals; they feel they are meeting their potential and are making a significant difference to the lives of others and to the organization.

A study of a more nuanced approach to the needs hierarchies models is worth our time. Frederick Herzberg posited a Two-Factor Theory of Motivation.[7] In this model, the bottom three levels are not motivators; they are hygiene or maintenance factors. People can have these needs met but only sufficiently to alleviate dissatisfaction. In other words, salary and fringe benefits don't motivate people or only to a very limited degree, but if they are not sufficiently met the employees may be dissatisfied.

The highest two levels of esteem and self-actualization are truly what motivates the workers. They may strive to eliminate or reduce the negative effects of the lower levels, but this doesn't motivate them to any significant degree. A sense of making a difference and meeting their self-established professional goals is what will motivate them to strive ever higher. So, as the theory goes, if a leader wishes to have motivated employees, they need to help them meet their own goals. This would seem to lend itself to an approach of self-motivation as the individual strives to meet their own goals and aspirations. Further, this concept is more congruent for the professional class of employees.

It is now worth a moment to circle back to Abraham Maslow. His later work (apparently unknown to many) expanded to include cognitive, aesthetic, and transcendence levels of needs (see figure 2.5).[8] The former two are immediately after esteem and just prior to self-actualization. It is this highest level, transcendence, which is most applicable to the principles herein.

People are most motivated when they are not self-actualized in isolation, but when they are transcended by values to be interconnected with nature and with others. This is where we get the most out of ourselves and the most out of our organizations—when we network and connect with one another to meet our common goals and mission. It is not a selfish self-actualization—it is beyond that. It is transcendent self-actualization with the whole. We must each ask ourselves how we could structure our organizations to support such a model of transcendent self-actualization. What would the congruent principles of motivation be for transcendence?

Michael Maccoby[9] described the interaction between the motivations of the leader and the motivation of those who are led, as described in figure 2.6. Such an interplay between the leader and those they lead is a potentially critical insight into the optimal approach required for employee motivation, or at least to understand why some leaders approach motivation the way they do.

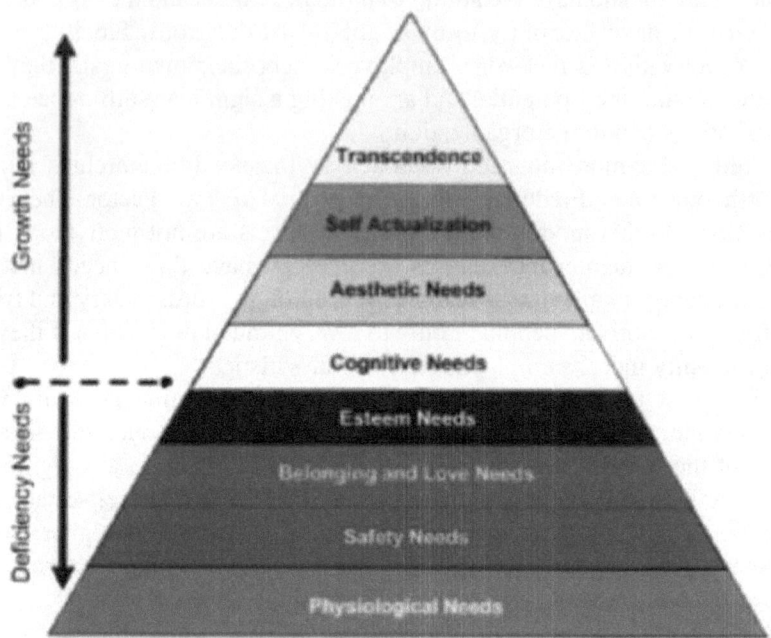

Figure 2.5 Maslow's Final Needs Hierarchy. *Source*: Saul McLeod, "Maslow's Hierarchy of Needs Hierarchy." https//:www.simplypsychology.org/maslow.html.

	Motivation of Led	
	Have to Follow	Want to Follow
Common Good	*Designer Persuades*	*Democrat Collaborates*
Motivation of Leader		
Personal Power	*Dictator Dominates*	*Demagogue Seduces*

Figure 2.6 Maccoby Leader/Led Motivation. *Source*: Michael Maccoby. *The Leaders We Need and What Makes Us Follow*. Boston, MA: Harvard Business School Press, 2007.

Those bosses who are more interested in personal power, corrupt an organization either directly as a dictator or through the insidious nature of a demagogue. As the old proverb states, "Power corrupts; absolute power corrupts absolutely." Some leaders are masters of persuasion toward a common goal. Still, they lead as a figurehead, and the success of the organization ultimately falls on their shoulders. If, however, the leader and the employees work together in a democratic collaboration, the mission stands on its own and its success falls on collective shoulders beyond any one person or singular point in time.

Reflecting back to chapter 1 and earlier in this chapter, it is prudent to ask oneself a series of questions. How do your leadership style and beliefs, and what you believe about people (Theory X or Theory Y), impact your view of motivation for your staff and team? How do your notions of employees as professionals and your beliefs in transformational leadership impact your approach to staff or team motivation? Who is responsible for motivation? What are your responsibilities as the leader? What are the responsibilities of the employees? Is your organization structured to support what we know best works for professional motivation? These questions will come back for a re-examination in the final two chapters.

So, what do you believe? What are the best approaches to motivate employees? What motivates you, and what approaches best work to motivate you? How do you motivate others? These are the precise questions we raised of elite coaches and athletes. Their responses to these questions are enlightening:

(1) What are the best approaches to motivating others?
(2) What has worked and not worked for you in terms of motivating others?
(3) What motivates you? And what techniques have you found best to motivate you?
(4) Do you supervise everyone the same way? Please explain.
(5) Do you think you work in more of a professional or a bureaucratic organization? Or is it a professional bureaucracy?
(6) Is motivation and leadership in athletics different from motivation and leadership in the professional world? In other words, are the skill sets and attributes for leadership and motivation transferrable from the athletic world to the world of education and to the corporate world? Explain.

THE INTERVIEWS

Vince Lombardi holds a place as an American motivational icon. He is best known for his fiery sideline rants and overtures. The Coach Lombardi of lore may not have been the person of reality in the locker room, however. This John Wayne mystique may have been more a Hollywood version of reality and missed the entire complexity of the man and the relationships he held with his staff and players. Lombardi cared deeply about his team, worried about them, and took care of their individual personalities when he chose how to approach each player's motivation.[10]

Before a leader even considers how they engage with others for motivation, they need to begin with themselves. Women's Volleyball Hall of Fame member and national bodybuilding champion Nicky Bowman explained it this way: "Know who you are, your values, your identity as a human-being, not just as a professional. Understand how you express your values to others and know your strengths."

These elite athletes and their coaches were asked what motivates them, and some of their answers might come as a surprise. Today's athletes have a drive to provide for their families. Many drew their motivation with their parents or grandparents in mind, according to Ann Lebedeff International Women's Collegiate Tennis Hall of Fame member. Former NFL star Harry Sydney explained, "I had a crazy childhood—lots of anger. I was fulfilled when playing football; it was the one place where everyone in our family was happy. It was the only time my parents paid attention." Gordon Marino added, "Luckily, I loved the gridiron arts and wanted nothing more than to play in the NFL, but there was another motivation, success in sports always made my dad loosen up and smile and I certainly wanted to please him."

Former NFL great Darryl Sims was straightforward. I wanted to be the best version of Darryl Sims I could be. I always wanted to be relied on to be able to do my job. If the coach said we need you to fill the D-gap, then I was going to be counted on to fill the D-gap. In college, I was motivated to excel academically—that was a promise I made to my mom, and I was motivated to excel in football. In both cases, I was going to be the best version of Darryl Sims I could be.

Another former NFL star—Evan Oglesby—had a different perspective. "I wanted to provide for my grandmother and my mother for all they did for me." In a similar vein, former professional baseball player Ralston Cash acknowledged, "I wanted to do well for my host parents, for all that they sacrificed for me." Nicky Bowman felt compelled to excel for she knew she represented her family and her community as a Native American woman.

Of course, each player is motivated to do well by their teammates, or at least to not let their teammates down, according to Larry Owens and Mike Hartman. But coaches like Owens and Jame Carney, Dick Stockton, Jeff Reinebold, Harry Sydney, and Evan Oglesby are now driven to make a difference in the lives of our youth and the younger players. Baseball star Ralston Cash expressed that he left baseball so he "could be the best possible father for his children."

Oftentimes, competition and challenge drive people. Again, Ann Lebedeff shared, "I always wanted to be the best at what I did—that motivated me." Mike Owensby added, "Tell me I can't do something, and I'll do it." Agreeing, Mike Plant explained, "I am motivated by the quest and to compete and to get others to do their best." Joshua Pickett added that he, too, was motivated "by competition pushing me to get better and by high energy. Intrinsic motivation drives you to be the best you can be." NFL player Juwan Green agreed. "If you need someone else to motivate you, then you're not a professional. It comes from within."

Gabby Smith Roethlisberger and Gretchen Rush agreed. In the words of Rush, "Competition is the best motivator; it's a natural motivator." When she competes in equestrian events, even today, Abbey Dondanville says she wants to perform better than she did at her previous competition—always working on self-improvement.

As time moves on, athletes and coaches mature and their drive and attention shifts; their motives can become more altruistic. Chan Gailey expressed it this way: "When I was younger, I needed to prove myself. When I became older, I wanted to make sure I was doing it the right way." Jeff Reinebold continued, "At my age it has changed. I don't need to prove anything. My time is limited; time is precious. I don't get too many 'bunches' of athletes to work with anymore. I focus on their development and reaching their goals."

Jon Reinebold noted, "I have a personal mission to give more than I receive—to serve others." To which he added, "You have to model the behavior. You can't win if you compromise your values." Evan Oglesby has created a foundation "designed to help get kids out of poverty by helping them use their skills to get scholarships." With respect to her native heritage, Nicky Bowman explained, "I wanted to honor the cultural value of my community by taking care of my body, to be drug-free to show kids what can be done."

Olympian Jennifer Demby expressed it this way.

> You have to be true to yourself. I was motivated by the competition. It was intrinsic. I wanted to excel and to achieve. That was rewarding to me and gave me a sense of pride. Now, co-founding and serving as a coach and director of Sports for Blind Athletes, Inc. is integral and gives me pure joy and happiness to advocate for the blind community.

Marcus Campbell said when he played, "I would have died on the field." Now that he has graduated into the community, his motivational focus is on giving back, for example, to St. Jude's Hospital.

Once a leader truly understands themselves and what motivates them, they can begin to focus on their followers. Three-time Olympic cyclist Sarah Hammer said it really depends on the individual, and you won't know what motivates them unless you ask. This requires that the leader "is supportive, a listener, calm, and quiet." NFL star Tavarres King provided an example. "Peyton Manning knew how to talk to the guys. He knew each of them as individuals. He made you think about yourself—about how you were doing. The best players and coaches build camaraderie, bonds, and relationships."

Former Olympic speed skater and current president of the Atlanta Braves Foundation Mike Plant said, "Listen to them so they know you are listening and hearing them—that you value their opinions and help them to take self-leadership." Sol Ross University head football coach Barry Derickson continued, "Build relationships; make it so they know you have invested in them. It's highly individualized. You need to help them build their own motivation and their own self-standards of success." Former college football player and present business owner Fred Roethlisberger added, "You need to get to know them as individuals. It comes down to a balance of support and challenge."

Former head college football coach and assistant to University of Wisconsin Coach Dave McClain, John O'Grady extended this line of reasoning. He emphatically stated,

> It is about building relationships. Each person is different. Simply put, you need to ask your players and assistants what motivates them. When I was a young player, I needed to be told what to do, but a fellow linebacker friend of mine couldn't handle that approach. We were so different.

As a player, Joshua Pickett felt that a combination of intrinsic and extrinsic approaches works. From a former player's perspective, Darryl Sims expressed that extrinsic motivation is problematic, however, because it's "not consistently reliable."

University of Maryland football star Dean Green said it takes a combination of team motivation and individual motivation. His coach would challenge the offense against the defense, for example, at practice. But he also built relationships with the players to understand what motivated them as individuals. "For me, I was always one of the best athletes, even as a child. I was motivated to be the best player on the gridiron."

From a head coach's perspective, CFL and college football coach Marcel Bellefeuille put it this way:

> There are two aspects: the physical environment (does it look and feel professional?)—which is often underappreciated, and the psychological—help them reach their own personal goals within the framework of the team's goals. I sit down with them formally three times per year and do this in writing. I do this with both my assistant coaches and athletes. People do want to improve their craft.

Two other professional coaches expressed the differences between the athletes of today and those of yesterday. NFL head coach Chan Gailey recalled the days of his youth.

> When I played high school ball you were motivated to represent your school and community. You did not want to let them down—we had school and community pride. Today's generation is all about family. I work with them to understand how they can secure and improve their next contract so they can best take care of their families.

Juwan Green knows he is a role model for his nephew. He wants his nephew to see his success and what it takes to be successful.

Milwaukee Bucks scout and former women's basketball coach at Western Michigan University, Ron Stewart agreed.

> Today's coaches need to focus on the players and their families. Family is extremely important to them! Coaches have to invest in their assistants and be committed to them. The Bucks have four officials who focus entirely on player enrichment. Financial motivation is a component. The players only have a short window to compete and to get the best from their talents and earn their salaries. That short window motivates them. They know how to prepare and how to compete—they're professionals.

Once the leader has built the relationships and knows what motivates their assistants and their players, they need to help them become self-motivated. Former college and NFL-Europe coach Larry Owens stipulated, "Find out how you can best help the person motivate themselves. I have found they are motivated to not let their teammates and coaches down."

In the words of Jame Carney, three-time Olympian and two-time world cup champion cyclist, "I can't be their motivator. You have to teach them to want it, to be their own motivator."

Professor and coach Marino agreed. "Once you know their goals, aspirations—their motivators, then you need to check in with them on a regular basis and ask them to ask themselves: Am I living up to the standards I set for myself?"

Another head football coach, for the new USFL Philadelphia Stars, Bart Andrus elaborated,

> I tell my players their game film is their resume. Then I ask them, "Did I do the best I can do?" This motivates them through visualizing their end performance. Your work toward perfection leads to excellence. You need to do it for yourself and for your team, not for your coach or you'll never get there.

Former lineman at Middle Tennessee State University and current high school teacher and golf coach Mike Owensby placed some additional responsibility on the shoulders of the coaches. "The coach needs to adapt their style to meet the needs of their players. Like any coach inherits a team, all leaders inherit a staff. You need to adapt to them." Owensby concluded, "Be positive. Negativity only gets minimal reward."

Former collegiate baseball coach and star player Jon Reinebold spoke of his own experience as a team leader. "The three levers you can use for motivation are: Autonomy, Relatedness, and Competence. People are motivated by being able to make decisions on their own, by gaining competence, and by building connections and relationships." These are the types of individuals former college running back Willie Garrett hires today—the person who is self-motivated and coachable. "I can give them increasing responsibility."

When starring on the University of Texas softball team Gabby Smith Roethlisberger learned too that motivation is individualized. With a nod toward Nietzsche, "People are going to do what they're going to do. Their 'Why' is different. Their 'Why' motivates them. The leader has to help them reach their 'Why.'" Jennifer Demby had a very similar take. "You have to listen. Athletes need to know their Why—their motivation. Then the How becomes tolerable."

Finally, as former collegiate baseball star and coach and now athletic director Jim Peeples explained, "You need to let them know you care." NFL cornerback Evan Oglesby explained, "You have to let them know you believe in them and express it. My coach empowered me by helping me understand what I could accomplish. He believed in me and trusted me." And in the words of NFL running back Harry Sydney, "You need to show them the possibilities and how they can do it."

Just as there are good strategies that help motivate individuals, there are approaches that squander opportunities. These coaches and athletes have seen them all. In many instances, bad leaders simply do the opposite of what the leaders above were just noted to do. They don't build relationships, don't get to know their colleagues, don't listen, and don't individualize, and "They don't communicate their expectations," according to Fred Roethlisberger.

Bad leaders lose track of their role in motivation. Gretchen Rush played professionally at Wimbledon, the U.S. Open, the French Open, and the Australian Open. She explained, "Nobody had to push me. I've been self-motivated my entire life; I'm a professional." The leaders who feel motivation is their responsibility often try to emulate approaches used by someone else. Again, Coach Gailey shared his thoughts. "You have to evaluate your own personality and follow that. Don't motivate like someone else. People can see through that. It doesn't work. And be honest!"

One approach to motivation that certainly does not work for professionals is any form of manipulation. Dick Stockton, former Wimbledon and U.S. Olympic tennis star noted, "Don't over-coach or over-motivate; you can't over-think." To which Mike Owensby added, "No cookie-cutter or one-size-fits-all approaches." Former Los Angeles Dodgers recruit Ralston Cash agreed. "Gimmicks and motivational speeches don't work."

Similarly, fear does not motivate professionals. "It causes people to over-think and make bad decisions," reported Bart Andrus. Gabby Smith Roethlisberger agreed, "Fear doesn't motivate. It only gets you so far. People need to know you care about them." "Brute force," doesn't work either according to Jon Reinebold. "That will only get you so far. Sometimes it might be necessary when time is crucial or lives are at stake—for example in combat, but it doesn't last."

The same can be said about overt criticism. Jim Peeples explained, "Poor leaders point out your flaws and what you need to do, which doesn't motivate." Green Bay sportscaster and former college lineman Burke Griffin added, "Most people don't like to be belittled in front of others," and such approaches won't work. "Complaining and yelling don't work," noted Jennifer Demby. "Praise in public and criticize in private," stipulated Chan Gailey.

Former collegewide receiver Marcus Campbell felt unreasonable punishment distracted from the team goals. "It's an abuse of power. These kinds of coaches eventually take the fun out of the game. They are antagonistic, divisive, and they lose any sense of brotherhood." Juwan Green concurred, "Those coaches who are abusive don't motivate. We are men; we are professionals—and we should be treated that way."

Praise is the one-time external motivation that can work. Harry Sydney explained, "Players like to be recognized in front of their peers. Small awards in front of their teammates makes a difference." Vince Lombardi was well known for fun little rewards. For example, he and his assistant coaches gave out $5 to players who "graded out" exceptionally well during each game. Bart Andrus made similar awards part of every week's team meetings.

From his experience, Coach Bellefeuille stipulated, "Authoritarian approaches do not work in the long-term. Furthermore, unrealistic transactional approaches don't work—where the carrot is too far out of reach. You have to be authentic; you must be yourself in your approach." It doesn't work "when a coach gets all up in your face. Yelling is one thing, but in your face is overboard," noted Duke University cornerback Joshua Pickett. Dean Green agreed, "Rah-rah coaches and screamers don't work, and neither do those who always point out the negative."

Is there a difference between motivation for athletes and coaches? When asked if they supervise their assistant coaches with the same approaches they do with their athletes, these coaches gave a variety of responses. For example, Chan Gailey explained, "Assistant coaches are different than athletes. You have to find out what their needs are—career or family needs." Dick Stockton concurred. "Assistant coaches are different than athletes.

You must find out what their needs are and what motivates them. Excellent assistant coaches are rare, but I've been very fortunate." Ann Lebedeff had a similar reaction to Stockton. "Most of my assistants were my former athletes. They were golden to me, because they served as the go-between for the players and me."

In a somewhat similar fashion, Larry Owens said, "Players are different than coaches. You supervise coaches to help them learn how to be prepared to help the kids." Extending this reasoning, Jim Peeples noted, "Each assistant has different goals and aspirations. You have to ask them and be authentic in listening and in your support." College basketball coach Jamie Purdy added, "Different approaches are needed for different assistants, just like for the players. I can delegate more to the experienced assistants."

Jon Reinebold had a very different view and responded through the lens of "Needs Theory" expressed earlier in this chapter. "People are people. Each are individuals and have different needs and motivators. It doesn't matter whether they're athletes or coaches." Because supervision and motivation need to be individualized, Bart Andrus held few large team meetings. Most of his work focused at the unit or individual level. In the words of Sarah Hammer: "Different approaches for different people—You need to create trust and provide guidance on an individual basis."

Abbey Dondanville expressed it this way: "I used to be more laissez faire, but that didn't work. Now it's more of a team effort and a web of relationships in mentoring new people; it's now individualized to each person's needs and context." Former college fullback Mike Hartman had similar experiences as team owner of a semiprofessional football team. One of his coaches needed regular direction, reminders, and support. Another was highly organized, prepared, and driven. The supervisory approach for each coach differed based on their own particular needs.

Working with assistant coaches segues into the topic of organizational structure. Are athletic departments, even teams, considered to have more professional or bureaucratic characteristics? Just as supervision of assistants varied among the interviewees, so too were these responses from the veteran coaches and athletes. Differentiation between the team and the department, or even the league, is critical for this discussion.

At the Division III level, the schools are typically smaller, budgets are dramatically leaner, and often the coaches and athletic department staff wear multiple hats. This is the level which most likely exhibits a professional orientation. Ann Lebedeff explained, "In DII and DIII the professionals wear so many hats, they run it and rely on each other. In DIII it's more of an academic focus." John O'Grady agreed that DIII is much more likely to be run by the professionals, and John has coached at DIII as well as at Wisconsin, Kent State, and Miami of Ohio.

Larry Owens, on the other hand, felt college athletic departments are becoming more professional bureaucracies or more Weberian. Coach Pat Cerroni agreed.

> At DIII it's really both. Running the team is a matter of survival every day—to keep the team afloat and moving forward. There are so many NCAA and conference rules and regulations that make it difficult. Still, coaches do have a degree of autonomy, so that is professional.

Gretchen Rush sees the same thing. "College athletics, and higher education in general, are becoming highly bureaucratic; it's really becoming a professional bureaucracy." Barry Derickson has coached at all three levels and feels that "it really comes down to the school and the leadership at the school. Some schools and some leaders are more professional and others more bureaucratic no matter the division."

In a somewhat concurring statement, with a hint of warning, John Roberts expressed,

> The best athletic departments are professional organizations. Unfortunately, DI is becoming too bureaucratic—we are too worried about checking all the boxes, filling out all the right forms, getting sued. It can whittle away at your soul. You have to put people together who care about the kids. You need a balance; bureaucracies begin to feed themselves.

Upon reflecting on her experience as an athlete in two different NAIA sports, Professor Abbey Dondanville suggested,

> One was very professional. The coaches had been professional athletes and treated the team professionally and organically. They were very adaptable. They didn't have aspirations to move on. Another coach was very bureaucratic—he had aspirations to move up, so he made sure we checked all the right boxes.

"DI softball was very bureaucratic, but our coach tried to protect us from it at Texas. There are so many demands, money, and NCAA rules and regulations," according to Gabby Smith Roethlisberger. "At Middle Tennessee State University athletics is a job. It's highly structured like a corporation," noted Mike Owensby. Again, John O'Grady, explained that DI athletic departments and budgets are so large that they have become massive bureaucracies.

Marcel Bellefeuille has coached at both the professional and collegiate levels.

> Well, bureaucracy is everywhere in large organizations. College is about process and gives you a certain degree of autonomy and flexibility. At the professional

level you have a little less flexibility, because the results-based approach is all about winning. But I've been fortunate to have had professional autonomy as long as my process fits within the vision of the organization.

Former DI and professional football star Even Oglesby put a fine point on it.

> Athletics is really a fraternity. When we meet a stranger who played the game, we know what they went through. We all put in the work, you know, the grind. It's a certain level of respect. A Brotherhood. A bond. At the DI and Pro levels, it becomes more about the money, so the bureaucrats have more influence, and you lose that sense of bond.

Oglesby saw the NFL as a professional bureaucracy. Harry Sydney agreed. "It's a professional bureaucracy and works when everyone understands their role." Bart Andrus, who served as a head coach in NFL Europe and the CFL and was an assistant in the NFL, elaborated,

> The pros are very much a professional bureaucracy. It depends on the franchise, though. You have to work through the league office. It is not a good system. The NFLE was much better. The focus must be on the players and what is best for them, not for the money. If you focus on the players, you'll get a better product, and the rest follows.

Ron Stewart said professional basketball "is a combination of both. The NBA has a strong Players Association, and coaches have a strong voice in the league." From a senior leadership perspective Mike Plant explained, "The Atlanta Braves are most definitely a professional organization. Not all MLB teams are the same. The organization hires professionals, never tells them what to do. We are empowered as professionals and entrepreneurs."

NFL head coach Chan Gailey concurred, "The pros are much more of a professional organization. The head coach surrounds himself with professional experts. I always wanted to be treated as a professional."

Tavarres King had a slightly different take:

> In the NFL, it differs from team to team. My own experience is that the Giants and the Broncos were very professional organizations. The league itself is very bureaucratic. It's getting more professional with the Players Association, though. The NBA listens and empowers the players more. The players have more voice in the NBA. In the NFL, the locker room is run by the players. In the front office the owner and management hire the coach and should let him do his job.

The Olympics is an entirely different entity. There is the overarching umbrella organization of the U.S. Olympic Committee which is made up of suborganizations representing the different sports (e.g., cycling, swimming, track and field, skating, boxing, and equestrian), and the list goes on and on. In cycling, for example, Sarah Hammer explained, "It's a professional bureaucracy, but our organization is moving toward a more professional orientation giving more influence to the professionals. The Olympics, on the other hand, is getting much more bureaucratic, because so much money is involved."

Speaking of cycling, men's cyclist Jame Carney noted, "It's definitely a professional bureaucracy. These are highly trained professionals, and that part of the organization works as a professional organization, but the rest of the system—the Olympics—is highly complex and structured like a professional bureaucracy."

Ultimately, at the most local, small, or unit level, athletics is run more characteristically as a professional organization. This would include DIII, perhaps DII, and the Olympic sports groups. As the organizations become larger, for example, the Olympic Committee, DI, and professional teams they exhibit had more characteristics of professional bureaucracies or Weberian systems. The NCAA, the International Olympic organization, and the professional league offices become more and more bureaucratic because of their complexity and enormity.

The final question posed to these elite coaches and their athletes was truly aimed at the premise of this book. Are the leadership and motivational attributes and lessons we have discussed transferrable to educational settings and potentially even to corporate America? Their answers did not disappoint.

Without exception, each athlete and coach were emphatic that lessons learned in sports can be applied to the work setting. Specific to higher education, Bart Andrus projected, "It is very much similar. Head coaches would make good college presidents. You can run any organization like a professional football team." Larry Owens did lend a sympathetic ear toward college administrators. "It's easier to coach college athletes. A chancellor once told me you have more power over the players. It is hard to supervise or have power over tenured faculty and unions."

Specific to the college classroom, Ron Stewart noted, "The best coaches are good teachers—they know how to teach." Coach John O'Grady who coached and taught a 6-credit load each semester concurrently said, "Certainly the organizational skills are transferrable, and so is getting to know and work with people. The professors are what the university is all about." Juwan Green explained, "Our coaches are like our professors. They prepare us for life outside of football or after college."

As a university professor now, Dr. Dondanville posited,

The skills and attributes are absolutely transferrable. As an employee, you want knowledge and comfort that your leaders are organized, have a plan, and are committed to it and to you. You want to be treated as a professional and not an automaton—it's about the personal, the intangible.

Jennifer Demby noted, "Most definitely. You learn discipline to continue with the work, to never give up, and a strong work ethic. You learn it's okay to make mistakes and time management skills."
Jame Carney continued,

There is definite cross-over. Competition helps in all aspects. It brings out the best in everybody. I became a better student because of competition. Challenge transcends sports and the workplace. You need to be empathetic and compete fairly. Leaders need to be able to check their ego in order to be successful as leaders.

Dick Stockton concurred,

The lessons are the same—to be self-motivated, to deal with adversity, to learn from mistakes through analysis, and to take a negative and make it a positive. You are always striving for constant improvement. Time management is huge; Jimmy Connors was the best. He taught me to use every minute wisely.

Mike Owensby had similar thoughts: "Determination, dependability, accountability, empathy: these life lessons are transferrable." Jeff Reinebold agreed.

The attributes are very much the same. Football reveals character and culture inside of the team and culture inside of family. It's about communication and honesty. Coach Dick Vermeil called it, "the gift of accountability." Our motto is: "don't attack the person, attack the problem." This means to affirm the person and provide the negative feedback to the position.

"Yes, these lessons are transferrable," according to Gretchen Rush. "The biggest one is you get a new day each day. For example, you get a new semester; you get new students, etc. Don't give up. Bring all that you have. Billie Jean King said, 'Champions adapt.'" Chan Gailey added, "Absolutely. People are people, and they all want professional autonomy."
Ann Lebedeff stipulated, "Yes, all the qualities are the same for leaders and for coaches and athletes—no matter the field. It's about your style in working with others, about communication—they all transfer over." Harry Sydney

noted, "It's all about life." He founded the organization *My Brother's Keeper*. Their values include the following: integrity, responsibility, accountability, and respect. Dean Green explained, "Successful coaches and athletes become excellent leaders in any organization. They are driven, have a tremendous work ethic, and know what it takes to be successful. People are naturally drawn to them."

Willie Garrett shared his perspective. "Absolutely they are transferrable. You lead by example. People are motivated for the next challenge. They need to be challenged like each new opponent in football." Evan Owensby explained, "We all want to be successful, so the leader needs to capture that. They have to make the job fun and motivational. The best leaders are successful in multiple areas." Ralston Cash concluded, "It's absolutely the same. Good coaches and leaders pull disparate players or groups together for a common cause."

University rugby coach John Roberts has also served as a college administrator. "In athletics and administration you need to set goals, determine how to measure them, and meet challenges and obstacles. Athletics teaches resilience and self-motivation. Athletics is a microcosm for work." Sarah Hammer added, "Companies like to hire top athletes, because they are 100% committed to a shared goal and they see it through."

Likewise, Marcel Bellefeuille explained,

> Yes, there is always something applicable. In both athletics and in the corporate and educational world it's about process, about environment, the psychology, and the culture. You need to invest in people, and to communicate your vision—what are the desired outcomes, and how will you measure them. Without these, it is only rhetoric.

Gabby Smith Roethlisberger said the attributes are 100 percent the same across athletics and the work world. "You need to be coachable and a team player." Fred Roethlisberger concurred, "It's about communication, interaction, playing your role on the team, and team dynamics." Roethlisberger's coach Pat Cerroni concluded, "The skills are absolutely the same. They are about listening, empathy, helping others win, and making relationships."

"The skills are incredibly transferrable," according to Athletic Director Darryl Sims.

> Team-work, handling success and failure, identifying the right people, work ethic—it's in our DNA. You meet people not like yourself but have one thing in common—a goal and you need each other to be successful. When I first arrived in Madison we had to come together. Those two-a-days were grueling. You build a camaraderie. You build team-skills, pulling for each other. That's

why Enterprise Rentals hires are 60% former NCAA athletes because of these attributes.

Sims concluded, "I am committed to myself and to my colleagues."
Football standout Marcus Campbell said, "These skills and attitudes are absolutely transferrable—without hesitation, in every aspect of life." Coach Jamie Purdy summed it up best. "Absolutely. Coaching and athletics apply to work, marriage, home life, everywhere." She added, "In the athletic department the AD doesn't need us to be 'yes-men.' He needs our input, our feedback, and our experience." Indeed, the best coaches and college administrators hire professionals, support them, communicate with them, and let them do their jobs.

CODA

The coaching carousel is much deeper and intertwined than many of us can imagine. Most coaches change teams frequently—very frequently. They move within their athletic conferences, across athletic conferences, indeed, across divisions. Some jump back and forth between college and professional ranks. It truly is a fraternity, and they know each other well.

A brief personal story is a microcosm of this feature of coaching careers and drives home the points discussed earlier about motivation. We've learned that motivation works best when it is individualized, supports and encourages self-motivation, and is built upon relationships, challenge, and support.

In 2009, Perry Rettig served as the associate vice chancellor for Academic Affairs at the University of Wisconsin Oshkosh. He had just finished playing semi-pro football in the area and joined the UW Oshkosh coaching staff as a volunteer assistant defensive line coach. Pat Cerroni was the Titans' head coach. John O'Grady had recently retired as the head coach at the University of Wisconsin River Falls and joined the Titans staff as an offensive coordinator. Barry Derickson starred on the offensive line for Oshkosh and Fred Roethlisberger for the defensive line.

The Titans were preparing to play their archrival University of Wisconsin Whitewater Warhawks. Whitewater was a dominant team in the league and has won several DIII national championships. Walking across the practice field on an early fall evening, Rettig asked O'Grady what was the difference between the best team in the conference and the rest of the teams?

Rettig expected it had to do with superior talent Whitewater was able to recruit out of the metropolitan areas of southeastern Wisconsin and northern Illinois. So, he was shocked to hear O'Grady's response which came startlingly quickly, "Whitewater's 2's want to be 1's. Most teams' the 2's are just happy to be on the team."

The 2's are second-string players, and the 1's are the starters. The 2's work hard to improve and to become starters. This not only makes them better but also pushes the starters to become better. The entire team becomes better. Other teams, according to O'Grady, have just as exceptional starters as the best teams; they simply don't have the depth of motivated 2's.

Coach Barry Derickson reminded Rettig that when a freshman tries out for a team, they are motivated to make the travel squad. Sophomores want to play or even start. Juniors want the accolades and stats, and seniors want to star and to win as a team. This concept roughly aligns with the Maslow's Needs Hierarchy model. Athletes' motivations change over time. Glickman's supervisory model is also important, here. As people's motivations and experience change over time, the supervisor's, or coach's, role changes with it.

Derickson discovered self-motivation as a player when he was mentored by Cerroni. Coach Cerroni adapted a "scope" model for his team. He personally taught the model to his assistant coaches, and each assistant coach was responsible for implementing it with their units. The scope focuses on self-motivation in the areas of football, family/social, academic, and spiritual. Goals are established in the realms of the personal, position, and team. At the center of the target is "Championship."

Each individual player was expected to set goals in each of the areas. Their positional coaches met with them routinely to discuss their goals, monitor progress, and make adjustments as necessary. Coaches and players alike ardently followed the program. The Titans eventually beat their archrivals and played in the national championship game. Cerroni finished his career with unprecedented success at the school. Many of his former players have continued in athletics serving in high school, college, and even the professional ranks.

*One final note: Rettig graduated with his bachelor's degree in Education from the University of Wisconsin Whitewater. As of this writing, Coach O'Grady now serves as special teams coach at the University of Wisconsin Whitewater. Coach Pat Cerroni has retired, and Barry Derickson is now head coach at Sol Ross University in Texas. Derickson continues to use the "scope" he learned from Cerroni with his own players. The "scope" is appended at the end of chapter 3: see figure 3.7, with permission from both Cerroni and Derickson.

NOTES

1. Douglas McGregor, *The Human Side of Enterprise* (New York: McGraw-Hill, 1960).

2. One of the key tenets of professionals is they hold themselves, individually and collectively, accountable.

3. Perry Rettig, *The Quantum University: New Knowledge Requires New Thinking* (Lanham, MD: Rowman & Littlefield, 2021), 13–15. Adapted from Joseph Luft, *Group Processes: An Introduction to Group Dynamics* (New York: National Press Books, 1970). Cited in Carl Glickman, Stephen P. Gordon, and Jovita M. Ross-Gordon, *Supervision of Instruction: A Developmental Approach* (Needham Heights, MA: Allyn & Bacon, 1998).

4. Henry Mintzberg, *The Structuring of Organizations* (Englewood Cliffs, NJ: Prentice-Hall, 1978).

Mintzberg expressed five different ways organizations are modeled, one of which is the professional-bureaucracy which serves as the focus for this chapter. Eventually, Mintzberg posited a sixth type of organization.

5. Abraham Maslow, *Religions, Values, and Peak Experiences* (New York: Penguin, 1970).

6. Lyman Porter, "A Study of Perceived Need Satisfaction in Bottom and Middle-Management Jobs," *Journal of Applied Psychology* 45 (1961): 1–10.

Cited in Glickman et al., *Supervision of Instruction A Developmental Approach* (Boston, MA: Allyn & Bacon, 1998).

7. Frederick Herzberg, *Work and the Nature of Man* (Cleveland, OH: World Publishing, 1966), 56.

Cited in Glickman et al., *Supervision of Instruction A Developmental Approach* (Boston, MA: Allyn & Bacon, 1998).

8. Abraham Maslow in Saul McLeod, "Maslow's Hierarchy of Needs," *Simply Psychology* (March 20, 2020), https://www.simplypsychology.org/maslow.html.

Cited in Rettig, *The Quantum University*, 80–81.

9. Michael Maccoby, *The Leaders We Need and What Makes Us Follow* (Boston, MA: Harvard Business School Press, 2007).

10. David Maraniss, *When Pride Still Mattered: A Life of Vince Lombardi* (New York: Simon & Schuster, 1999).

Vince Lombardi and W.C. Heinz, *Run to Daylight* (New York: Prentice Hall, 1967).

Chapter 3

Organization for Success

Whether you are a coach or an athlete, or whether you are a school superintendent or a college president, you will have a preferred approach and philosophy of leadership. Similarly, you will have motivation strategies and beliefs which you will employ for those people in your organization whom you lead. At the same time, all leaders work within an organizational structure, whether inherited or self-created, which they use to help maximize their leadership and motivational approaches. It will be interesting to see the organizational structure elite coaches and athletes find themselves in and even more if the models fit their belief systems.

Chapter 3 will commence with a brief review of the extant literature of traditional models of organizational structure. These are the models most of us grew up in. They may be all that we know; they may have become our mimetic isomorphism—the way we do things because that's all we know and have experienced. The literature review will then turn to review the emerging or more contemporary theories of organizational structure. The newer sciences and democratic principles and values will serve as a basis for much of this work.

As with the previous two chapters, this chapter will then shift to the interviews to find out what today's leaders in the world of athletics say and have experienced. It will be quite interesting to see if their beliefs about leadership and motivation are best supported by the structures within which they work. Coaches and athletes spend a great deal of time reflecting on principles of leadership and motivation, of course, but little time is spent considering organizational structures and the ways they impact the people who work within them. This fact made for some rather exacting and prosaic dialogue at times.

Chapter 3

THE LITERATURE

Most of us are quite familiar with the traditional top-down hierarchical approach to organizational management. It is the model we were taught and most likely what we cut our teeth on. As a matter of fact, it is likely the model we continue to experience today. Before moving too far into the literature, it is worth a quick review of the underlying assumptions of our classical model.

In our nation's preindustrial era, organizations were more simply structured and built to be flexible around the workers and the straightforward tasks at hand. Bureaucratic leaders did not exist and did not get in the way of worker autonomy. This all changed with the advent of the industrial revolution and the war complex. Systems became too large and complex for simplistic organizational structures. A formal model of organizing and leading our systems was needed. Our leaders turned to science.[1]

The classical sciences, believe it or not, formed the basis for our past and present conceptualizations. The closed model of Newtonian physics was founded on linear, mechanistic thinking. The foundation of this science was a simple study of the parts of the system in a reductionistic fashion in order to understand the whole, studied in detail, and enabled to be put back together. For the purpose here, the key principles of classical sciences are the following: (1) Objectivity, (2) Reductionism, (3) Linear determinism, (4) Control, (5) Replication, and (6) Prediction. It was a clockwork universe. The machine became the metaphor. Frederick Taylor provided the scholarship.

The formal study of organizations focused on efficiency, consistency, and control. Industrialists believed they could run their institutions like the machines they made. French industrialist, Henry Fayol, explained that management had five major functions: planning, organizing, commanding, coordinating, and controlling. Management had truly become a science. Those at the top ran the system, the well-oiled machine.

Max Weber, however, was concerned about too much power in the hands of the few. To mitigate his concern, he turned to the highly structured bureaucratic model wherein power would be diffused among the many objective-minded and highly trained professionals. The result was the omnipresent pyramid model we all know today, with senior administration at the top of the pyramid, middle management in the middle, and the workers at the bottom. Patrick Dolan[2] modified this model for K-12 schools. (See figure 3.1 Dolan's K-12 Education Governance Model.)

The three circles and the top of the pyramid represent the board of education, the executive—superintendent, and the teachers' union. The middle portion of the pyramid represents the central administrative units of the district. The bottom portion of the pyramid represents the individual schools in the district

Organization for Success

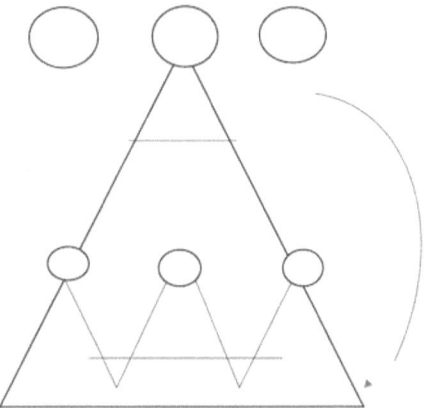

Figure 3.1   Dolan's K-12 Education Governance Model.

with a principal at the top. Along the outside of the pyramid is a sweeping arch. It represents advisory groups (e.g., PTAs).

This has been subsequently adapted by Rettig for higher education (see figure 3.2 Higher Education Governance Model).

The premise of this bureaucratic model was to provide for precision across functions and a highly trained professional class with specific responsibilities and knowledge. Lines of authority and communication were clear, decision-making was precise and not arbitrary. Anyone who has worked within such a model knows, however, what may be visualized in an organizational chart may not be reality. Such a model can be confining, ignore informal structures, create low morale, stifle creativity, and produce legalism. *Most important, the model is built on the assumption that the person on top of the pyramid knows more than those lower down on the pyramid.*

This discussion takes us back to chapter 2 where we discussed four organizational types: Chaotic, Bureaucratic, Professional, and Weberian. Most readers of this book will find themselves working in a combined model of bureaucratic and professional, or Weberian. Such a professional-bureaucratic model tries to capture the best features of both professional organizations and the structure of bureaucratic organizations.

Most athletes and coaches, as well as educators, find themselves working in such Weberian organizations. The rub, however, lies in the fact that the bureaucratic structure follows the notion that the individuals further down the pyramid know less than their "superiors." If indeed, however, the organization employs professionals throughout, the bureaucratic structure constricts their professional autonomy—by design.

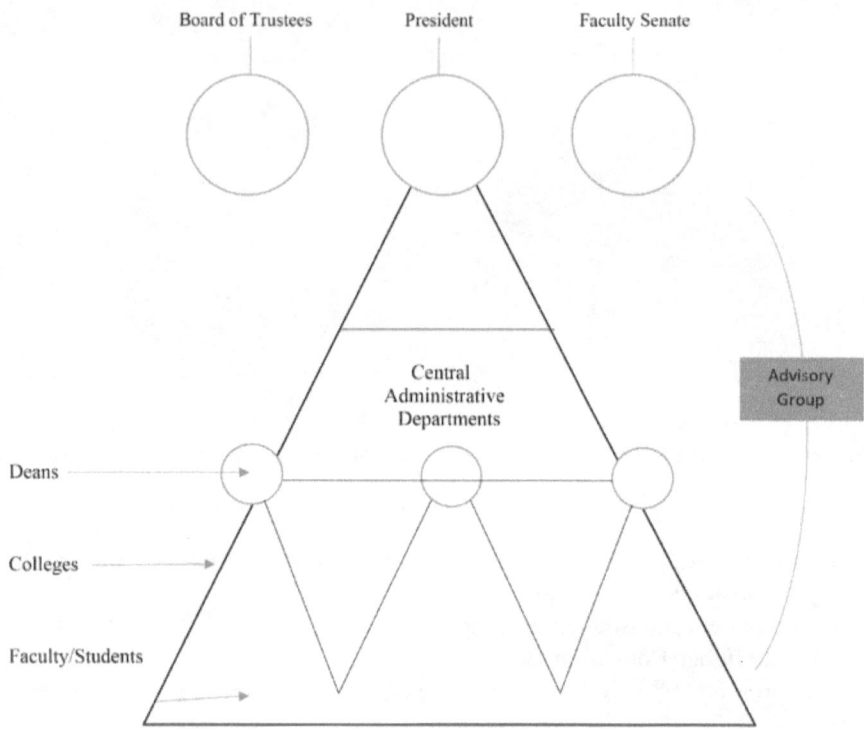

Figure 3.2 Higher Education Governance Model.

Of course, there are many people who believe our organizations are not nearly as tightly structured—tightly coupled—as the organizational charts and job descriptions would make them appear. These traditional organizations have the *appearance* of tight coupling, that is, they have clear and solid lines of authority, communication, structure, and policy. Rather, they believe our organizations are loosely coupled.

According to Karl Weick, loosely coupled organizations are more the rule than the exception.[3] This type of system is no better exemplified than in higher education where a professional class of entrepreneurial and highly independent thinkers is loosely connected to one another on a day-to-day basis. Leading such an eclectic group is more than difficult—ask any college president.

The contention of people who believe our organizations are loosely coupled is that these systems only have the *appearance* of tight coupling. For example, in the lead up to the Normandy invasion on D-Day, General Eisenhower had Army engineers and Hollywood technicians build canvas and papier-mâché tanks and other materials which were placed miles away from the intended landing zones on Omaha and Utah beaches. The appearance of a strong Allied buildup far from the actual plan forced Germany to divert many of its troops and preparations to the wrong location.

These systems, especially universities, are less rigidly structured and monitored in reality than we have been led to believe. Lines of communication are fluid and little real formal supervision or monitoring takes place. These organizations rely on an informal structure, have unclear goals, and often appear chaotic or messy. At the same time, they are adaptable and may be highly effective, and they rely on a highly educated professional class. In fact, faculty governance was established as a way for the professors to police themselves—to hold themselves to account.

It would be interesting for the reader of this book to critically reflect on their own organizational structure. Is its reality more tightly or loosely coupled? Is it highly professional relying on the ethics and training of a professional class, or is it more highly organized and led by a bureaucratic class? Or is it perhaps a combination of both—a Weberian model? A similar reflection is warranted about the reader's notions of the employees in their organization? Do they exhibit more Theory X or Theory Y characteristics? Should their colleagues be considered more professional or bureaucratic? How do the organizational structure, policies, and protocols influence this? Chapter 4 will examine these questions.

Perhaps the traditional view of our educational institutions is wrong. Perhaps they are more loosely coupled than the old models suggest. Perhaps they rely on a professional class and informal structure more than we understood. Perhaps our employees are more Theory Y workers who want to be engaged, are self-motivated, and care about their collective mission. Would a different organizational model be warranted? If so, where would we look for direction? Perhaps the model already exists in nature. Perhaps it has already been adapted by our founding fathers.

It has been Rettig's conjecture that nothing is wrong with Newtonian physics. The science is robust, but its application to our organizations is misplaced. If we were to look to the sciences for a model, rather than look to Newtonian physics, we should look to quantum physics and the other newer sciences. For example, biology, keystone processes, chaos theory, fractals, the human brain, black holes, and holograms might provide us clues.[4]

Two brief examples from the newer sciences might go a long way in helping to understand how science can provide us direction. The first comes from the science of Keystone Species, and the second from Quantum Physics.

While organizational theorists use a pyramid model to depict a system's bureaucratic structure, ecologists may also use a pyramid model, as well. This pyramid depicts plants as the base of the pyramid, predators on the top, and plant-eaters in the middle (see figure 3.3). In higher education, organizational

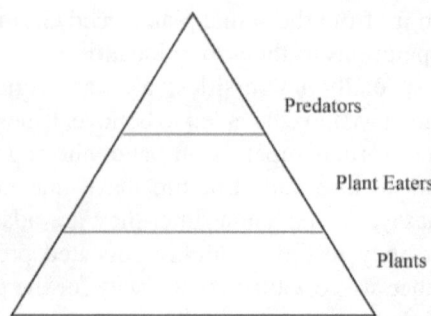

Figure 3.3   Ecological Pyramid Model.

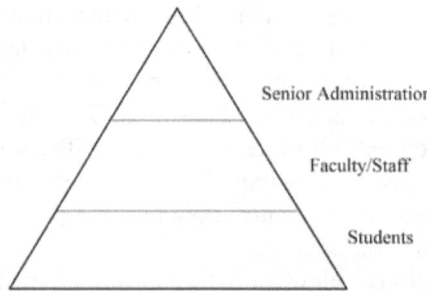

Figure 3.4   Higher Education Organizational Pyramid Model.

theorists denote this pyramid model with students at the bottom, senior leadership at the top, and faculty and staff in the middle (see figure 3.4).

While the parallels may not be clean—students and plant-eaters, and senior administrators and predators (are qualitatively different—thankfully)—the overall schema remains the same. In October 2019, the Public Broadcast System (PBS) premiered, "The Serengeti Rules" on its *Nature* show. The program was based on the book of the same title by Sean B. Carroll (2017).[5]

"The Serengeti Rules" explored the emerging concept of "Keystone Species." The father of this concept was Dr. Bob Paine, a zoologist at the University of Washington. He noticed that by completely removing the predatory starfish from a protected ecosystem—a tidal pool—the mussels (plant-eaters) took over and destroyed all the plant life since no predators were there to keep them in check. The rigid impermeability of the tightly controlled system might not have been real, as will be seen later.

So, rather than looking at the pyramid from the bottom-up, he saw that removing the predator, the top of the pyramid, had the largest impact on the ecosystem. Removal of other layers in the pyramid did not have the same devastating impact on the system. Thus, Paine discovered that some species are more important than others; he coined these species, "Keystone Predators."

The metaphor struggles a bit, here. Are we saying that those at the top of the pyramid are the keystones of the system? Are senior administrators more important than the faculty—those who are central to the mission of the institution? Are they more important than the students without whom the organization would not even exist? But the research wasn't finished.

This body of research saw a profound shift under the work of Dr. Tony Sinclair, a zoologist with the University of British Columbia. He studied ecosystems in the Serengeti of East Africa. He found that significant reduction of wildebeests—plant-eaters—made the greatest negative impact on the ecosystem. This caused predators to die off, as well as overpopulation of grasses. Therefore, predators were not the Keystone, but rather plant-eaters were the Keystone. He thus coined the term, "Keystone Species to explain this phenomenon."

This research suggests that any layer in the ecosystem pyramid could be the Keystone—the most critical layer of the pyramid. Extending this lesson to the higher education organization metaphor, that would suggest any layer may be the Keystone. Still, could we say that the faculty are more important than our students, or that students are more important than faculty, staff, and administration? The metaphor is strained once again.

Perhaps there are not Keystone *Species* but rather Keystone *Processes*. Rather than say a particular species or layer is the critical *species* of an ecosystem, maybe a *process* is the critical aspect. For example, perhaps the process of renewal is the critical aspect of a natural ecosystem. The normal state of nature is to seek a state of equilibrium, or homeostasis. In order for homeostasis to exist, the system continually balances each layer against the others. If one layer or level sees significant declines, the other levels get too large, and the system ultimately fails and dies. It is as if nature has its own system of checks and balances.

Now the metaphor works for our education organizational structure. Rather than looking for a critical layer in the pyramid, we should look for a critical process—a process that creates a system of checks and balances. In colleges and university settings, for example, that system or process which best ensures checks and balances is shared governance. Both the natural ecosystem and the higher educational organization system process for checks and balances are depicted in figures 3.5 and 3.6.

When the system of checks and balances provided by shared governance is disrupted, the entire system becomes fragile and weakens; it may even perish. Shared governance provides each layer in the organization the place and opportunity to voice its concerns and ideas, keeping the other layers in check. Remove faculty authority or student voice, and senior administration may grow too powerful for the system and result ultimately in a weakened institution.

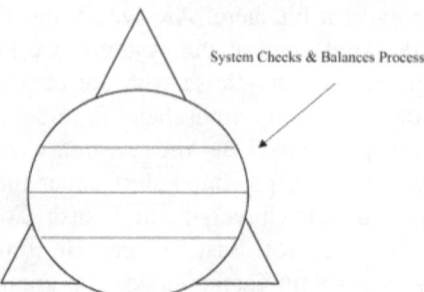

Figure 3.5 Ecological Pyramid Model with Checks & Balances.

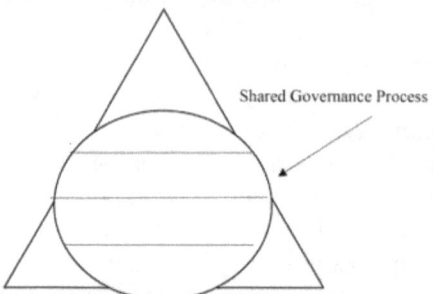

Figure 3.6 Higher Education Organization Model with Checks & Balances.

Without faculty checking, the authority of their administration or board of trustees and the integrity of the institution are threatened. There then comes a tendency for external groups to dictate the curriculum, the mode of instruction, and perhaps even the quality of students. This change makes the health of the system untenable. As faculty become fearful for their jobs, students may see lower quality in instruction and expectations, and faculty become the hired hands of those making the unilateral decisions.

On the other hand, a too powerful faculty will potentially seek stasis in an environment needing to change and adapt for survival. In this sense, faculty can deliberate the system to a slow death. Conversely, too much emphasis on student wants and students as customers can find an organization arbitrarily chasing new trends, seeking the lowest common denominator, and losing its original focus or mission. Again, a system of shared governance checking and balancing each layer keeps the institution fit and adaptable.

Does a system of checks and balances exist in the athletic domain? Is it necessary? Is there a keystone layer or a keystone process in these organizations? Has one group become too powerful and unchecked?

Other lessons can be learned from quantum physics and chaos theory. When natural systems want to maintain harmony, they seek equilibrium. At times natural systems, however, move away from equilibrium as they seek innovation. Innovation and creativity are the only way they can survive—they must adapt. "Chaos is ubiquitous in natural systems."[6]

What's more, "We now know that far from equilibrium, new types of structures may originate spontaneously. In far-from-equilibrium conditions we may have transformation from disorder, from thermal chaos, into order."[7] Chemists and physicists Ilya Prigogine and Irene Stengers explained that what might appear to be disorder or chaos, really has an underlying order. What the organization's leader needs to do is allow for the actual underlying order to appear, to emerge.

Margaret Wheatley explained, "As chaos theory shows, if we look at such a system long enough and with the perspective of time, it always demonstrates its inherent orderliness."[8] We humans only are able to see a small portion of the system in terms of time and space across the organization at any given moment. We do not see the system working in its entirety. We are not trained to do so.

Nonequilibrium is actually a source of order. As Prigogine and Stengers so eloquently stated:

> In many cases it is difficult to disentangle the meaning of words such as "order" and "chaos." Is a tropical forest an ordered or chaotic system? . . . Nevertheless, the feeling persists that, as such, the overall pattern of a tropical forest, as represented, for instance, by the diversity of species, corresponds to the very archetype of order.[9]

The science of complexity has taken the next logical step beyond chaos theory and has been applied to evolution, ecology, biology, computer science, and economics.[10] This science talks about interweaving relationships and networks, and about equilibrium, or the status quo, as a sure sign of death.

The Santa Fe Institute in New Mexico is a fluid think-tank of some of the most brilliant minds in the world in physics, in economics, in politics, and in other fields. The scientists in the social fields know that their sciences cannot be reduced to simple linear formulas and algorithms as has been attempted in the past. They know that real life is far too complex for such simplistic thinking. In his writings for real-life application of the science of complexity, Michael Waldrop explained, "These complex, self-organizing systems are *adaptive*. . . . Species evolve for better survival in a changing environment—and so do corporations and industries."[11]

The Santa Fe Institute has closely analyzed the science of complexity and the lessons that can be learned from chemistry, quantum physics, and molecular biology and how these lessons can be applied to complex organizations and systems. Capra and Luisi describe characteristics of biological life[12]—which have already been shown to have parallels to organizations. Waldrop went on to cite the work of John Holland, computer scientist at the University of Michigan. In Waldrop's words:

> Holland started by pointing out that the economy is an example of "complex adaptive systems." In the natural world systems include brains, immune systems, ecologies, cells, developing embryos, and ant colonies. In the human world, they included cultural and social systems such as political parties or scientific communities.[13]

Clearly, administrators choosing to tightly control their organizations in tough times may actually be squeezing the life out of their systems—a very ironic twist. The purposefully rigid pyramidal hierarchies stifle adaptability, creativity, and the lifeblood of the professional organization.

Waldrop shared one final real-life example of complexity science in action. Change can happen slowly and incrementally over time, or change can happen abruptly in an instant—like a tornado or a fire. This is known as punctuated equilibrium, where change can happen very quickly and out of control. In a university, an academic department may slowly adapt its curriculum or abruptly change to a new delivery method, for example, online instruction. Institutional reaction to Covid-19 was a prime example.

A football team might have a star athlete go down to injury, or a new offensive coordinator may come in with an extremely different scheme. Change can happen abruptly even to a static pyramid model. Nobody feels in control, then. Oftentimes, administrators overreact to this sense of losing control and squeeze tighter with more policies and protocols which becomes a vicious cycle.

Without going into the agonizing detail of the rest of these sciences, the lessons of our contemporary sciences are clear:[14]

- Organizations are like living natural systems.
- Communication is the lifeblood of an organization.
- Systems need a process of internal checks and balances to keep the whole in balance.
- In order for systems to live, they must adapt, change, and create.
- Equilibrium may be the sign of death of a system; disequilibrium can create renewal.
- Control might squeeze life out of the system.
- What might appear to be chaos might actually be order. Indeed, sometimes order comes from chaos.

- Change can be slow and incremental, or it can be abrupt and punctuated.
- Small perturbations or disturbances can have a huge influence anywhere in the system.
- We must look at the system as a whole, over time and space.
- Communication with feedback loops across the system is critical.

Margaret Wheatley may have summed up these lessons best:

> Here is the real world described by new science. It is a world of interconnected networks.... In this highly sensitive system, the most minute actions can blow up into massive disruptions and chaos.... When chaos erupts, it not only disintegrates the current structure, it also creates the conditions for new order to emerge.... This is a world that knows how to organize itself without command, control, and charisma.... Self-organizing evokes creativity and results, creating strong, adaptive systems. Surprising new strengths and capacities emerge.[15]

Are our institutions built for adaptability, for loose coupling, for swift communication, and for professional creativity? Have we provided for keystone processes—processes of checks and balances? Are we comfortable with what at times appears to be chaos? To where do we turn for the answers?

Perhaps a model in our society already exists—one that is congruent with these lessons of the newer sciences. Our founding democratic values and principles just might be that answer. In chapter 1, we discussed one leadership model as "Democratic." What would that look like in an organization? Of the original founding ideals of our nation, there are five core democratic values and four constitutional principles which may be applied to our educational organizations.[16]

Democratic Values

- Liberty: personal freedom, free flow of information and ideas, open debate, and freedom of assembly.
- Common good: greater benefit for all, majority rule while protecting the rights of the minority.
- Justice: fair treatment, shared decision-making.
- Equality: no class hierarchy.
- Diversity: diversity and representation of both the people and of opinions.
- Honesty, Openness, and Fairness: in all interactions with each other.

Democratic Principles

- The rule of law,
- Checks and balances,

- Separation of powers, and
- Representative government

The four constitutional principles, in higher education, are conceptually met through the responsibilities of the three governance pillars: board, executive, and faculty senate. The principle of *the rule of law* is primarily established through the codification of policies and bylaws; nobody is held to standards outside expectations as formally established.

The principle of *checks and balances* and *separation of powers* are most notably met through delineated responsibilities associated with the respective pillars—board, executive, and faculty senate. The principle of *representative government* is met through the faculty senate, and possibly staff councils and student government associations.

To be clear, representative governance does not infer that every person or group votes on every topic. In the words of Olson, "Shared means that everyone has a role. . . . 'Shared' does not mean that every constituency gets to participate at every stage. Nor does it mean that any constituency exercises complete control over the process."[17] This example would closely mirror a Weberian organization as a delicate balance between the professional and the bureaucratic.

University of Southern California Professor Christopher Boehm noted, according to *Washington Post* reporter Sally Jenkins,

> "followers subtly rule hierarchies. . . . Pyramid shaped organizations tend to be constructs." According to Boehm, "we devised them early in human history—not to promote tyrants but for the sake of efficiency: Someone had to organize and lead the hunt. When leaders abuse that grant of authority . . . groups can have brutal ways of dealing with them, leveling mechanisms that range from ostracism and shaming to even execution."[18]

It will be interesting to see if our elite coaches and athletes perceive their organizations to be more organic and natural or more static and traditional. Are they highly structured and authoritarian/bureaucratic, or are they more professional and democratic? Are there three governance pillars? Are governance principles of, say, checks and balances established? Or even more difficult, do they try to lead with one model that might not fit the organization in which they work?

Now it is time to hear from the coaches and the athletes themselves. Do they work within a highly rigid and static structure—the kind stereotypically associated with athletics? Or do they have a different model, one that is more nimble, natural, and dynamic—one that utilizes democratic principles? If so, what does it look like? Is there a difference between the structure of the organization and the structure within the actual team—the locker room?

Whatever the system they work in, does it work effectively? What are its strengths and weaknesses? Even more important, does the structure support their beliefs and approaches to both leadership and to motivation? Here are the questions for this portion of the interviews:

1) Describe the part of the organization you lead—teammates, team, and organization.
2) Do you play a formal or informal role in this structure's leadership? Which role is most effective or impactful?
3) Is it the traditional hierarchical pyramid? Where do you fit in the pyramid?
4) Do you have a different model—one that is more democratic or organic? Describe.
5) How effective is the model? What are its strengths? Its weaknesses?
6) Does the structure support your leadership approach? What about your motivation approach? (This question was wrapped into the other previous questions posed to the interviewees.)

THE INTERVIEWS

The first and third questions posed to the athletes and coaches were simply to establish context. Would answering the questions from the perspective of athlete or coach, individual or team sport, make a difference? Did having a role in administration of an athletic team or after an athletic career had ended make a difference in their answers? Quite frankly, in the end, none of these perspectives made a substantive difference. The responses were similar across all groups. Of course, even team athletes spend a great deal of time preparing on their own. All the coaches, and even the administrators, were athletes earlier on. So, their experiences did not alter the facts of their perceptions.

While the responses to the second question were surprising, they should not have been. These elite athletes and coaches have very strong feelings about where their greatest impact comes from. While their formal roles are necessary, for the most, their greatest influence truly comes from their informal relationships with their peers and their staff.

Still, University of South Carolina rugby coach John Roberts stipulated, "It starts out with the formal role. They will listen because of your position and your reputation. Once you have established that relationship, your bigger influence comes from the informal side. But your reputation is vital—it's your brand." Former head football coach at the University of Wisconsin River Falls John O'Grady concurred, "The greatest impact comes from your informal role. However, we start with the formal team meetings, but then we break down into position groups. And on the field, it's much more informal and individualized; it's about those relationships."

The University of Ottawa head coach Marcel Bellefeuille agreed with O'Grady. "As a head coach, I play more of a formal role—within the framework of the full team. The informal comes at the individual level and by the assistants. Formally, I set the standard and the culture." Olympian Jennifer Demby shared her perspective. "It starts from the formal side of being known and respected as the coach. That's what they call me. It's about respect for the position."

Gabby Smith Roethlisberger, former University of Texas softball player, explained:

> Definitely informal. The head coach is certainly a formal leader. My coach knew his techniques and strategies, but his impact came from his informal side by building relationships with the players and their families. He built trust! The biggest thing he gave us was his time.

NFL coach Raheem Morris was a tremendous informal leader according to Juwan Green. "No matter who you were on the team, he built a personal relationship with you."

Former Middle Tennessee State University lineman Mike Owensby agreed. "Coaches play both a formal and an informal role. The love for their athletes is informal. Respect needs to go both ways—you're a role-model." Duke University football standout Joshua Pickett noted the informal role of his high school coach Benji Harrison. "Coach Harrison played an impactful informal role for me. He genuinely cared about your life. It wasn't all about football." (An interesting side note: On the day of this interview, Joshua had just returned home for Winter Break. After the interview he was headed out to have lunch with Coach Harrison.)

Former San Francisco 49er and Green Bay Packer Harry Sydney explained it from a different perspective.

> It simply depends on the person. Some are more formal and some more informal. In the huddle, the quarterback is the formal leader, but there are the informal positional leaders. Everyone is talking amongst themselves between the plays, but once the quarterback steps into the huddle everyone stops talking and listens. In either formal or informal situations, the best leaders listen, are able to respond quickly, and then make decisions.

Athletic director at Piedmont University and former baseball coach Jim Peeples expressed it this way:

> While I have a formal role, of course, most of my success comes from the informal role I play. I help them find the best of every opportunity. You need

to build relationships with students and their families. Your words and actions need to be congruent—you are a role-model. The kids see it. Quite frankly, too many higher education administrators don't know their students and can't relate to them.

Chan Gailey served as the head coach for the Dallas Cowboys, the Buffalo Bills, and the Georgia Tech Yellow Jackets. In his view, "A head coach is a formal role, but I tried not to use it too much. Most of my leadership was informal. It gets better results." Former U.S. boxing coach Gordon Marino noted, "Teaching and coaching are the same thing. It takes both a formal and informal role. You have to be comfortable in your own skin and not rely on only the formal side."

Fred Roethlisberger played football collegiately at both Northern Michigan University and the University of Wisconsin Oshkosh. He explained that a coach's informal role was the most crucial. He gave the example of the impact his coach had on him, his brother, and his family with a heart-to-heart conversation about what it would take to make the team and earn playing time. "Coach Cerroni pulled me aside and looked me in the eye. He allowed me to be vulnerable. I needed his honesty and to be able to share my personal thoughts."

Bart Andrus served as head coach for NFL Europe Amsterdam and the CFL Toronto Argonauts and now the USFL Philadelphia Stars. He relayed what he learned as an assistant to Jeff Fisher with the Tennessee Titans and St. Louis Rams and with LaVell Edwards at Brigham Young University. "The coach's informal role is the most impactful. It's about developing the individual relationship and family. Coach Edwards and Coach Fisher did it because they cared."

Former Olympic and professional tennis star and now head coach at Hollins University, Gretchen Rush noted, "I get the most impact from my informal role. It comes from relating to my players and my assistants and by building trust." LaGrange College football star Marcus Campbell expressed it this way: "The informal role or relationship helps the creative side. My best coach gave certain informal team leaders the 'green light' to lead their teammates. We had the freedom of input to say what we thought would work and what wouldn't."

It should be clear by now that these elite coaches and athletes are emphatic when they state the biggest impact comes from their informal leadership role. However, are the systems in which they work structured to best support this informal role, or are they organized with more formal roles in mind? Conventional pyramidal and hierarchical models are built for a formal organization. Informal organizations are built more naturally to support organic and dynamic decision-making and interactions; they provide for more democratic processes to thrive.

However, such an apparently clear-cut structural dichotomy implied by a rigid pyramid or an organic and democratic model may miss the mark. It is just not that simple. The larger organizational model may be structurally organized with the bureaucratic pyramid in mind, but as one moves closer to the players on the field or on the court it becomes much more organic, dynamic, and democratic.

"It's a pyramid," according to Fred Roethlisberger.

> It works pretty well. But it really depends on the personnel involved—the leader. It doesn't matter what type of organizational structure you have—it comes down to the people and how they work together. The leader has to be the glue holding all the parts together.

Gabby Smith Roethlisberger, who played softball at the University of Texas, explained,

> Some decisions can only be made by the leader or the boss. If your team is capable of making decisions or giving voice, then they absolutely should. If they have experience and expertise to share, the organization needs them to do so.

Gretchen Rush shared some interesting insights as both a player and as a coach.

> An athletic department is definitely a pyramid, and as the coach I'm on top of the pyramid of my team. A team is a pyramid within the athletic department pyramid within the university's pyramid. Structurally speaking the model works, but it is limited when it comes to excellence and the team-level. The pyramid supports and maintains stability, but excellence and professionals need more. They need more ownership, autonomy, and flexibility.

Chan Gailey directly stated that bureaucracies in athletics are not designed for excellence. Gordon Marino said, "Athletics have become too bureaucratic! They are not as effective as they could be." Retired college and NFL Europe coach, Larry Owens, explained, "We all work within a pyramid model. But there is not enough support workers or staff to make the model work effectively."

As noted earlier in the literature section of this chapter, the pyramid model is built with a critical assumption. It assumes that the person at the top of each level is more expert and knowledgeable than those people below. This assumption is crucial for the model to work, and it does not naturally assume those workers below are professional experts. Larry Owens went on to stipulate, "You need to surround yourself with people who know more than you in their own area. You need to hire professionals."

Former Olympic and professional cycling athlete and coach, and current university coach Jame Carney continued,

> For the Olympics there is a divide between the athletes and coaches and the Evil Empire/Administration. There is a big divide between the two. Coaches protect the athletes from the out-of-touch bureaucracy and the leaders who know nothing about the demands on the athletes. The coaches act as a buffer, so the athletes can focus on their profession.

(See the footnote at the end of this chapter for a description of the organizational structure of the Olympics from the IOC down to the individual sports bodies.)[19]

Jon Reinebold has played baseball at the U.S. Military Academy at West Point, coached collegiately, and served in special operations in Qatar during the Iraq War and as a battalion commander in Japan. He explained a very unique perspective from the military.

> It's very much a pyramid model, of course. The top of the pyramid precisely describes the mission and the end result, but the Army uses "mission focused orders," or orders that tell you the desired end state without dictating how to achieve that end state. It needs and relies on the professionals on the ground to adjust and make decisions immediately based on the circumstances and their training. They have professional autonomy.

The same can be said about the athletes once the game begins. A couple of plays may be called in the huddle, but the quarterback adjusts based on the defensive he is confronted with. The linemen adjust their blocking schemes depending on what they see. Receivers adjust their routes depending on man-to-man or zone coverage, for example, and running backs read the zone blocking schemes as the play unfolds. The players know the plan, but they must adjust on the run, quite literally. They have the autonomy to make decisions on their own and as a unit.

For that matter, the same can be said in all sports. This explains why Olympic and professional tennis star and college coach Dick Stockton explained, "You can't over coach or have players over think. The game is too fast for that. They need to be able to react naturally on their own." Those types of decisions are fluid and organic.

Finally, these coaches were asked if there is a place for democratic decision-making in athletics. In other words, are democratic principles and values applicable to the world of coaches and athletes? If so, how? If not, why not? Can you provide any examples? At first, the answers might come as a surprise. But when listening to their examples and reasoning, the responses appear to be congruent with their earlier answers about leadership and motivation.

Besides the one coach who exclaimed, "You gotta be kidding me! Are you out of your mind? We don't vote," the coaches and players were quite affirming in the need for democratic decision-making. To be clear, we are not talking about voting, although voting could be a part of it. For example, a coach won't ask the team to vote on which play to run or who should start. But they can use democratic values and principles elucidated at the beginning of this chapter. Still, this coach's comments were more than a little humorous.

Gordon Marino put it this way: "If you [athletic directors/administration] want coaches to open up to you and share what they really think, you have to create a culture where they can't be blamed. Vulnerability scares away trust. Most teams don't have this culture." On the other hand, Atlanta Braves Foundation president Mike Plant expressed, "From the management side, it's about building and protecting a culture of inclusion and diversity." These are democratic values.

Olympic-level equestrian competitor Abbey Dondanville added,

> The principles and values are absolutely democratic. Everyone needs to be genuinely heard, understood, and be seen. In other words, they need to be able to demonstrate their skills—to be seen—by their coaches. This is true not only on the practice field but during competition, as well.

Coaches and athletes have their own unique perspectives. Former head coach Bart Andrus said that decision-making is "democratic to the degree that everyone discusses the best approaches. Everyone must be on the same page. It is the responsibility of the head coach to get everyone there, and he makes the final decision." Evan Oglesby played in the NFL and said that while it "can be democratic, you need a coach to make the final decision. But the coach needs to know what the others think."

Head coach John Roberts had a similar view. "Sometimes you just need the coach to make the decision. But the players need ownership in the decision if they are expected to carry it out. They will fight for it if they own it." Roberts added, "They need to give feedback about the execution of a play. If they feel they can't execute it the way it is designed, their input will be invaluable in how to make it work."

In a concurring opinion, former head coach John O'Grady noted,

> There is a place for it [democratic processes], but ultimately the head coach makes the decisions. At staff meetings on Sunday afternoons, we decide

together. You gather their expertise, learn from them, and make your decisions. On the field, the players can make their decisions based upon options you taught them.

At the time of the interview for this book, O'Grady was preparing to meet with his punt return unit. He and his staff had prepared three return options which he was about to explain to the players at the special teams meeting. The idea was the players needed to understand the three options. Once the ball was snapped, they would need to decide which of the three options they would take based upon how the circumstances unfolded. They would need to make the decisions on their own and communicate with one another—instantly and on the run.

Head coach at Sul Ross State University Barry Derickson had a similar take.

> At the end of the day, it's still the coach's decision, but you have to hear your assistants out. I need 100% input from them and from the players. For example, I can tell a quarterback how we want to run a pass play, but if he's uncomfortable with how it is put together, he might throw an interception. So, I need to listen to him, and we'll make the necessary adjustments together.

Likening democratic processes to natural processes, Coach Bellefeuille explained, "Team leadership and organization is organic in how decisions are made and processes work. The democratic processes have strengths in that they bring out people's views and ideas—that's a necessary part of process." Darryl Sims added his view on democratic processes.

> Yes, our staff meetings are democratic—I can make the decisions by myself, but I need to hear from them and be inclusive. We reach better decisions that way and then everyone owns those decisions and are responsible for them, together.

Former baseball coach Jon Reinebold was emphatic in his use of democratic processes. "It's very democratic. Professional autonomy is a requisite in making decisions. But people need to be trained in how to get there." Head coach and now athletic director Jim Peeples was equally insistent.

> We're democratic in everything we do. We hash it out and collectively decide how to move forward. The other coaches have insights and expertise. We can't afford blind loyalty to the person. We need loyalty to the position, to the program. Too many administrators brown nose, which is not good for the boss or the organization.

In a similar vein, former head coach Dick Stockton added,

Yes, we're very democratic! We discuss which will be the best line-up and matchups, and we try out different approaches. It takes a great deal of trust with assistants and the coach. We need excellent assistant coaches. We capitalize on one another's strengths. They are experts in certain areas and have different experiences.

Chan Gailey was unequivocal when asked if he used democratic processes.

Very much so! If I tell my assistants, "These are the plays we're going to run," they won't be invested in them. We design and decide together. We have to be able to explain why. If we can't explain it to the players, then the players can't understand and carry it out. It's not about who is right; it's about what is right. This leadership is organic in that everyone can bring up topics or take the lead. Many young people have new ways of thinking and experiences, and they bring diversity.

Recently retired head football coach Larry Owens spoke from the heart and years of experience.

We've always been very democratic. When I was an assistant, I always just wanted to be heard; then, I could go along with the group decision. Whether I was coaching for NFL-Europe or college ball, we would challenge each other. We argued all the time; this capitalized on all of our strengths.

Owens explained,

I believe in the 51% rule. At the coaches' meetings we would argue about the plan for the next game. I needed the assistants to use their expertise and experiences and share their thoughts. We'd hash it out together. At the end of the day, I would be responsible for making the final decision. Ultimately, though, we came to the decision together. By doing it that way, everyone felt heard, the system was better, and they could agree to carry out the plan together. Their voices were heard.

While democratic processes make a great deal of sense at the coaches' level, and the examples just mentioned prove the point, can these same principles and values be applied to the athletes and teams themselves? The professionals seem to think so. Juwan Green explained that in the NFL, the coaches know the athletes are experts and confer with them during the game to determine what they are seeing and what adjustments need to be made.

Milwaukee Bucks scout Ron Stewart shared,

> The NBA has a strong Players Association. They are conferred with regularly. With respect to coaches and other management, the Bucks General Manager actively seeks counsel from everyone on his staff. Staff and players alike have a voice.

Former NFL player Tavarres King concurred, "There's a place for democratic decision making on the team. If you trust and respect certain players, then you will seek their advice. This is especially true on the field during the game."

Ralston Cash played pitcher for the Los Angeles Dodgers organization.

> I believe there must be a level of democratic decision making in athletics through captains, for example. On the field, it's very hard to win with a dominating coach. Players need to make decisions during the play. For instance, when a ball is hit to the outfield an infielder can redirect the throw as a cut-off. Just like in a business, when a company gets too influenced by one dominant individual, the organization gets out of balance. In my career, the two best coaches who were in-tune with the players and had that crucial balance were Damon Berryhill and Bill Haselman. Both coaches produced best record teams in my career. You went to war for them, and they for you.

Again, a case for democratic principles can be readily made when working with professional athletes. Does the same hold true for college teams? Fred Roethlisberger said, "Yes," with a caveat. "There can definitely be a place for democratic decision making if the team is ready. A freshmen-heavy team might not be ready, but if there has developed a strong senior leadership on the team, they can handle it."

Coach Pat Cerroni explained,

> I struggle with this very question every day. Today's student-athletes don't respond well to authority or tough coaching as in the past. They want to be heard. Their parents never provided discipline, so they aren't prepared for it. Authoritarian leaders can't be effective today. When it comes to decision making on the field during the game, it's very democratic. Today's offenses are so complex. They have three plays called every time they go up to the line. The defensive players have to adapt quickly; it's very difficult. The players have to make decisions on the field during the game. In team meetings and in practices we help them prepare to make those decisions.[20] (figure 3.7)

In his autobiography, *Run to Daylight*, Vince Lombardi wrote, "To play with confidence a team must feel that everything possible has been done to

Figure 3.7 Cerroni Adaptation of Leadership/Motivation "Target." *Source*: Cerroni, Pat. UW Oshkosh Titans: Titans Football 2021 Power Point presentation to Team. (@summer 2021), Oshkosh, WI.

prepare it fully for the coming game and there is nothing more we can tell them."[21] Indeed, Lombardi was known by his players to be "worthless" during the games. The control was no longer in his hands—it was now in the hands of the athletes. He had done all he could throughout the week, and now it was up to them.

Dean Green of the University of Maryland noted his experience with democratic decision-making followed the chain of command. Elite athletes' voices are critical. They share their thoughts with the team captains who share with the coordinators up to the head coach. Dean added another dimension. "College athletes are looked up to by so many people on campus. It's important that they become leaders, to serve as role-models, and to give voice to the people."

John Roberts continued, "I truly believe in democratic processes. There is a place for it, especially for today's athletes. When we were young, we did what we were told. That's no longer true. Coaches are democratic in that they need to listen to their players." Mike Owensby, former player and current high school coach, added, "Absolutely. Give them options and let them choose. They need to make decisions based on risks and rewards. These skills need to be taught, and then we need to put them in the best position to be successful."

Professional and Olympic cyclist, and now coach Sarah Hammer, when asked if there is a role for democratic decision-making responded, "I think so. Athletes' rights; Athlete Advisory Councils—both are important. Coaches can bounce ideas off of them." Former college basketball player and now coach, Jamie Purdy noted,

> It depends on what you mean. When I put in a new offensive or defensive play, before practice I will pull in a few players, and we'll try it out. We'll discuss how it works for them and make adjustments. In the game I'll ask them what they're seeing so we can make adjustments on the run.

Collegiate and professional tennis star, and now coach, Ann Lebedeff said, "Every player needs to have a voice. I have to make the final decisions, but I need to hear their opinions." Gretchen Rush added, "We are definitely democratic. Give them a voice. Empower them. You need trust. Give them value. We hold each other accountable. Democracy doesn't always work, and it is difficult and messy, but it's necessary." This message was delivered by Coach Rush throughout her entire interview—the message was clear.

The higher up you go—the more elite the athletes become—the more democratic it is. "You're respected for your experiences and qualifications. You are more empowered and listened to." Now, Jennifer Demby asks her athletes, especially considering they're blind, how to implement certain techniques. "How can I help you improve?" Her best coach was a thinker, and they helped her become a thinker—empowering her to make her own decisions.

Finally, Jame Carney expressed his view.

> I'm democratic. We decide together on which races to compete in. I ask for opinions. Sometimes I have to be the hard-nosed guy. They need to know they can't compromise other teammates' races. I just changed our spring schedule because over the break, I reached out to the team about the projected schedule. We made a major switch for our downhill athletes. This created a few more adjustments but now, we have a better schedule for everyone, and everyone feels heard and valued.

Further, Carney noted that "everybody deserves to be treated equally. Also, college students turn over every couple of years. Upperclassmen tell younger athletes how things are done around here." Carney also spoke of his assistant coaches. "I need to defer to them often. A head coach could be missing something, so deferring to their expertise is necessary. They are experts."

Indeed, these experts tell us democratic processes, principles, and values not only work but are also imperative for success. These coaches and athletes may work within quasi-bureaucratic structures that may behave more as loosely coupled systems, but they have professional autonomy and a culture of team.

NOTES

1. For a thorough review and analysis of the history of the classical sciences and the development of classical organizational theories, please refer to: Perry R. Rettig, *The Quantum University: New Knowledge Requires New Thinking* (Lanham, MD: Rowman & Littlefield, 2021).

The following several in-text paragraphs of historical description are borrowed from *The Quantum University*.

2. Patrick Dolan, *Restructuring Our Schools: A Primer on Systemic Change* (Kansas City: Systems & Organization, 1994). Cited in and adapted by Rettig, *The Quantum University*, 2021.

3. Karl Weick, "Educational Organizations as Loosely Coupled Systems," *Administrative Science Quarterly* (1976): 21.

4. Rettig, *The Quantum University*, 2021. In this book, Rettig goes to great length to describe, in layman's terms, these newer sciences and how their lessons could be applied to our educational settings. The following discussion of Keynote Species, Quantum Physics, and Chaos Theory come directly from this previous work. It is beyond the scope of *Trenches*, however, to provide any detail about these other sciences. For a much clearer review, the reader is asked to consider reading *The Quantum University*.

5. Sean B. Carroll, *The Serengeti Rules* (Princeton, NJ: Princeton University Press, 2016). "The Serengeti Rules." *Nature*. Video of the Public Broadcasting System. Edited by Benedict Jackson. Executive Producer: David Guy Elisco, Jared Lipworth, and Fred Kaufman. Produced by David Allen and Gaby Bastyra (October 9, 2019). Based on the book by Sean B. Carroll, The Serengeti Rules. Princeton, NJ: Princeton University Press (2016).

6. Jeffrey Satinover, *The Quantum Brain: The Search for Freedom and the Next Generation of Man* (New York: John Wiley & Sons, 2002), 203.

7. Ilya Prigogine and Isabelle Stengers, *Order out of Chaos* (New York: Bantam Books, 1984), 307.

8. Margaret Wheatley, *Leadership and the New Science: Learning about Organizations from an Orderly Universe* (San Francisco: Berrett-Koehler, 1994), 21.

9. Prigogine and Stengers, *Order out of Chaos*, 169.

10. Jeffrey Satinover, *The Quantum Brain: The Search for Freedom and the Next Generation of Man* (New York: John Wiley & Sons, 2002), 204.

11. Michael Waldrop, *Complexity: The Emerging Science at the Edge of Order and Chaos* (New York: Simon & Schuster, 1992), 11.

12. Fritjof Capra and Pier Luigi Luisi, *The Systems View of Life: A Unifying Vision* (Cambridge, United Kingdom: Cambridge University Press, 2014), 345–346.

These include:

(1) A living system is materially and energetically open; it is a dissipative structure, operating far from equilibrium. There is a continual flow of energy and matter through the system.
(2) It is self-organizing, its structure being organized by the system's own internal rules.
(3) Its dynamics are nonlinear and may include the emergence of new order at critical points of instability.
(4) It is operationally closed—an autopoietic, bounded network.
(5) It is self-generating; each component helps to transform and replace other components including those of its semipermeable boundary.
(6) Its interactions with the environment are cognitive—that is, determined by its own internal organization.

In such a system these authors add, "The web of life is a flexible, ever-fluctuating network. The more variables are kept fluctuating, the more dynamic is the system, the greater is its flexibility, and the great is its ability to adapt to changing conditions" (355).

13. Michael Waldrop, *Complexity: The Emerging Science at the Edge of Order and Chaos*, 145.

14. Rettig, *The Quantum University*, 62.

15. Margaret Wheatley, *Leadership and the New Science: Learning about Organizations from an Orderly Universe* (San Francisco: Berrett-Koehler, 2000), 170.

16. Perry R. Rettig, *Making Shared Governance Meaningful* (Lanham, MD: Rowman & Littlefield, 2020).

17. Gary Olson, "Exactly What is 'Shared Governance'?" *The Chronicle of Higher Education* (July 23, 2009), 2.

18. Sally Jenkins, "Keys to Good Coaching," article in the Washington Post. Carried in the *Atlanta Journal-Constitution*, December 26, (2021), 42.

19. Former U.S. Olympic cyclist and medal winner and member of the U.S. Cycling Board of Directors, Jame Carney explained the overall structure of the Olympics:

> The large umbrella group, of course, is the IOC—the International Olympic Committee. Each country has its own National Olympic Committee. The United States has the USOPC—the United States Olympic & Paralympic Committee. Under the USOPC the US has over 40 sport NGOs—National Governing Organizations. For example, Jame Carney sits on the USA Cycling board. In the past, some of these were referred to as federations.
>
> The IOC and the USOPC are largely corporate bureaucracies, according to Carney. The athletes, the professionals, are represented on AACs—Athletic Advisory Committees across these different groups. This provides somewhat of a system for checks-and-balances. The athletes, the professionals, are more highly represented on the NGOs.
>
> Mike Plant, former US Olympic speedskater has served on both the Cycling and the Speedskating NGOs, as well as the former USOC, and the USOC Athletes Council. Sarah Hammer now coaches and serves as an administrator for USOP Cycling in Colorado.

20. Fred Roethlisberger played under Coach Pat Cerroni. Cerroni very purposefully prepared his seniors, over their previous three years, to take on the leadership mantle for the team. Cerroni developed a leadership curriculum that has been widely viewed by and adapted by other coaches. The leadership framework for that curriculum is shown below.

21. Vince Lombardi and W.C. Heinz, *Run to Daylight* (London: Prentice-Hall, 1963).

Chapter 4

Putting It All Together

The previous chapters have provided a descriptive overview of the literature in leadership, motivation, and organizational structures. The theoretical foundations established a necessary framework for interviews with elite coaches and athletes at the collegiate, professional, and Olympic levels. These coaches and athletes shared their experiences and their thoughts around these three critical areas.

Each chapter's academic review concluded with the narratives provided by nearly forty athletes and their coaches. This final chapter pulls each of those chapters together to provide a clearer picture, a fuller picture, if you will. In other words, what can we learn from their stories? Can a singular model coalesce the concepts of leadership, motivation, and organizational structure? Can leaders be congruent in their leadership, their approaches to motivation, and to how they structure their organizations?

THE FINDINGS FROM CHAPTER 1—
ELITE LEADERSHIP

All coaches and college presidents or school administrators would consider themselves leaders and not managers. According to Kotter, leaders establish direction, align people, and motivate and inspire their workers.[1] None of these descriptors is in doubt. How people lead, motivate, and align is the rub. What makes them excellent leaders?

The leader's fundamental belief about their employees or their players is pivotal. Do they believe people are lazy, unmotivated, indolent, individualistic, and need to be directed (Theory X)? Or do they believe people are professional, hard-working, team-oriented, and self-motivated (Theory

Y)? This critical belief must ultimately drive the leader's approach to their work—how they lead, their approach to motivation, and how they structure their organization. Such a foundational orientation and understanding of people, indeed, becomes the pivotal nexus for all leaders.

According to the extant literature many leaders have certain traits or attributes such as intelligence, self-confidence, determination, integrity, sociability, charisma, emotional intelligence, values, and specific virtues. Others lead by the kind of work or processes they employ such as technical skills, human skills, and conceptual skills.

From the interviews with over three dozen elite coaches and athletes, we have learned that the leaders they have most admired express both special traits and process capabilities. Oftentimes, such differences are difficult to distinguish or isolate. For example, the most impactful leaders were said to be relationship builders and great communicators. They of course had qualities of intelligence, organizational skills, high integrity, and standards of ethics. These are men and women who are consummate role models and care about their charges as individuals. They are professional and treat others as professionals.

Many of these coaches are considered servant leaders who have a tremendous work ethic and the ability to pull others toward a collective and shared vision. They establish standards and hold themselves and those around them accountable. They most often have a calming influence and make others around them better. While they hold formal positions of leadership, they prefer to not rely on their authority. Their greatest impact comes from an informal relational approach. This creates either a collegial or mentoring relationship with their assistants or players. For the most part, these influential leaders have a Theory Y orientation.

These men and women are honest, forthright, steadfast, dependable, and adaptable. Their dispositions and attributes are contrary to those leaders who hurt their team or organization. Those are the leaders who treat everyone the same, are volatile, and don't build relationships. They are manipulative and egocentric. They are not people of integrity; they micromanage, and they treat others not as professionals but rather as human resources. Quite frankly, they have a Theory X orientation.

At times the literature will describe a leader by their power or authority. Authority is considered more in terms of formal position and legal. Power, on the other hand, is the ability to influence others. It can be either formal or informal. There are five sources of a leader's power: Referent, Expert, Legitimate, Reward, and Coercive. Those whose power comes from people liking them are considered to have referent power, and those whose power is derived from their expertise are of course considered expert. Legitimate power is from the formal position.

Reward power comes from the ability to reward others, while coercive power comes from the ability to punish or withhold reward. Reward and coercive power are considered the least effective. Legitimate power is effective to varying degrees. Relational and expert powers are considered the most resilient, and the research suggests expert power is the most efficacious.

Our interviewees felt the coaches obviously have formal power based upon their position or reputation; however, the most impactful power comes from influence and informal forms. Formal power or authority can get the coach in the door, but it won't take them far. Their real power comes from the relationships they establish, their expertise, and from the common vision, standards, and accountability they communicate.

Their power comes from bringing people together, empowering the professionals they lead, nurturing their professional and personal development, and creating a sense of culture. At times, they even consider power to be an illusion. All said, their real power would be considered referent and expert.

Some scholars focus on styles or on approaches to leadership. Eight primary styles predominate: Democratic, Laissez-faire, Pacesetting, Coaching, Autocratic, Servant, Transactional, and Transformational. Democratic leaders follow a set of shared and established principles, values, and norms. Laissez-faire leaders prefer a hands-off approach, pacesetting leaders establish outcomes and goals and hold their charges to account.

Leaders who follow a coaching style give direction and support to those they lead by minimizing weaknesses and building on strengths. Autocratic leaders tell their employees what to do and how to do it in a traditional hierarchical top-down approach. Transactional leaders use forms of reward, punishment, and manipulation to encourage employees to carry out their responsibilities. Transformational leaders and servant leaders develop a culture of supportive relationships and are mission-driven. They focus on shared vision and professional empowerment across the organization.

Oftentimes, of course, leaders are not singularly beholden to one model or approach. They are more likely to follow a situational style dependent upon their followers' needs or the particular set of circumstances in which they find themselves. These unique circumstances and needs require different approaches to their leadership and supervision. Such approaches are fluid from time to time, from situation to situation, and from person to person.

The coaches eschew transactional, autocratic, and laissez-faire styles of leadership. Such approaches are not professional and would hold a Theory X belief about their players and assistants. Of course, the coaches and players interviewed would see pacesetting and coaching as important methods, but they know servant, democratic, and transformational approaches are more likely to create excellence and ultimate success. Such approaches indicate a fundamental Theory Y belief in their colleagues.

As a matter of fact, these are the qualities they use to measure their own success. Both the coaches themselves, and their players alike, judge the leader's success by how well they build relationships and teach life skills and dispositions to those in their charge. They ask, did the coach develop both individuals and the team? Did each improve? Are the players and the team living up to their potential? Are they a positive influence on others? Do they help others become self-directed and self-disciplined?

Depending on the level, wins and losses are important, but the record is often considered a means to an end. Coaches can't impact others without having a record of success on the field, track, or court. If you don't win enough, you won't be around to influence others. The best leaders develop a culture of success focused on the people and on the mission. They are people of high integrity who build relationships and vision toward a common goal. They believe the best in people, challenge themselves and others, are role models, and have a professional orientation.

Are these leaders born or are they made? Those who favor the former belief are more likely to follow "trait theories." In other words, they believe that leaders have inherited some innate dispositions as noted earlier. Often books are written about prototypical leaders, those with particular traits, who have inspired followers. Other books are written about how to make leaders describing what skills or "processes" they utilize. Academic programs are built around these constructs.

From the interviews, we learned that most leaders are not born. While they may have some innate talent, or the "It Factor," those qualities need to be developed and honed. This parallels the description of a natural athlete who still spends hours in the gym or after practice, often alone, working on their skills. They have some inherent talent, but it must be developed.

The majority of those interviewed believe that leaders are made. At times, they are formal or informal students of leadership and soak up all they can by observing other leaders or from academic coursework. Others are thrust into circumstances that require their leadership. In either case, they learn from their mistakes and step up to the challenges. These emerging leaders practice their skills, focus on relationships, and focus on mission.

Do the best leaders in athletics feel it is best to be feared or loved? Without equivocation, the answer is loved. Fear only enters the picture in terms of not letting teammates, coaches, or family members down. It's alright to have opponents fear them, but they don't want to be feared by their colleagues. Fear is short-term, short-sighted, and does not garner excellence. The use of fear comes from a Theory X orientation.

Love is respectful, relational, and professional. It comes from a Theory Y orientation. Love is about building bonds, relationships, and teams. It is about integrity and believing the best in others. Love has the greatest impact on any team, it is sustaining and long-term, and it lives throughout the organization's culture. At times, our athletes and coaches said it all really comes down to mutual respect.

THE FINDINGS FROM CHAPTER 2—
MOTIVATION AT THE HIGHEST LEVEL

Today's leaders often have two ways to look at employee motivation. They either think it is not their responsibility and disabuse themselves of any such notions, or they think they do an excellent job of inspiring and galvanizing their team toward a collective aim. The topic of motivation is near and dear to the hearts of elite athletes and their coaches. How do they look at this critical concept? What do they see as the role of the coach and of the individual athlete?

Just as in chapter 1, we found that a grounding in how leaders view their colleagues—whether through the lens of Theory X or Theory Y—is critical in determining their approach to leadership, it is just as critical to determining their approach to motivation. The fundamental principles of motivation for athletes are readily transferrable to the corporate and education worlds.

Those coaches and organizational leaders who hold a Theory X belief about their athletes or workers believe their charges need to be motivated, persuaded, and even manipulated to perform and to strive toward accomplishing the overall goal. Theory X managers believe it is their responsibility to motivate the others. They must drive the system, reward and coerce, bargain, and cajole. They use a combination of carrots and sticks; they expect and they inspect.

The proponents of a Theory Y posture, on the other hand, view team and organizational motivation principles through a different lens. They see motivation as a cultural ethos breathing throughout the entirety of the team or system. They understand their colleagues are highly trained and motivated professionals who possess an inner drive toward excellence and success. They are self-motivated and find extrinsic approaches bothersome or even condescending. The elite professionals thrive on empowerment and a collective transcending approach.

These professionals begin with themselves. They are introspective and are cognizant of their own values—personal and professional. Often, they are motivated by a sense of altruism. Sometimes, early in their careers, they wish to make certain their young families are provided for and secure. They may want to repay perceived debt to their parents or grandparents, or to at least honor the sacrifices they made for them. Later in their careers, these elite coaches and athletes are motivated to help others whether they are younger players, the success of the team, or members of the community. They get a sense of fulfillment by helping develop the talents of others to meet their own goals, dreams, and aspirations.

At the height of their careers or during their greatest success, these athletes have been motivated by being members of the team. They want to help their team succeed, to be a part of that success, and to not let their teammates down. Of course, quite often, the most elite athletes are driven by competition and the challenge itself. In this manner, they are motivated to improve themselves, better their own skills, or improve upon their own personal records. They are driven to be the best version of themselves they can be; it is about self-improvement.

A leader's philosophical depiction of their team or staff will likely determine how they structure team or organizational dynamics. While this is the emphasis of chapter 3, its central features are critical to how leaders approach motivation. Some leaders, as noted earlier, prefer a hands-off approach to employee motivation. This laissez-faire orientation results in what Max Weber termed a "chaotic organization." These organizations falter and do not find success. In athletics, these coaches lose their jobs. Without any direction, there is no Theory X or Y stance—the system is rudderless.

Still, other leaders feel motivation is their responsibility; it is a problem needing a solution, and they own it. They create "bureaucratic" systems according to Weber. Their aim is to set goals and standards and forms of accountability. From these aims, they devise processes to reward and coerce, to drive and steer, and to hold employees to account. These are bureaucratic organizations with a clear Theory X viewpoint. Such teams and organizations find minimalization at the cost of standardization.

Those leaders with a Theory Y belief of their athletes or staff understand the individuals they employ are intrinsically motivated. Weber determined these "professional" organizations have an ethos or a culture of excellence, individual drive, and collective determination. Motivation is seen not as something that needs to be done to people, but rather as an emergent phenomenon embraced by an esprit de corps owned by both the individual and the unit.

Of course, most leaders have not been sufficiently introspective with regard to their beliefs about those with whom they surround themselves. Either that, or their organizations have become too complex and large to satisfactorily control (still a Theory X orientation), or they simply have inherited a bureaucratic framework. In either case, they may work in a "Weberian" system—one that has both professional and bureaucratic tendencies. Such a mixed model can lead to frustration by both the leader and the group—with a sense of incongruence. In the words of Gordon Marino, the people can have a sense of "cognitive dissonance." They're professionals working in a bureaucratic world.

Cognitive dissonance is real, and it is felt by people throughout the organization who feel they are being manipulated. The coaches and athletes are quick to describe what strategies don't work. Just as each person must recognize their own values and beliefs, they can see when their leaders are inauthentic and manipulative. Canned speeches and cookie-cutter one-size-fits-all approaches simply don't motivate.

These are highly motivated individuals with professional attributes and expertise. As such, they don't like to be treated unprofessionally, especially by bureaucrats who don't understand their work. Humiliation and demeaning leaders are not only off-putting, but they sink morale. Professionals, all people for that matter, should be praised in public and corrected in private. Fear and intimidation create animosity and will ultimately backfire.

Athletes will not respond well to coaches who don't communicate expectations, don't listen to them, and don't build relationships. College and professional football coach Marcel Bellefeuille stipulated, "Authoritarian approaches do not work in the long-term. Furthermore, unrealistic transactional approaches don't work—where the carrot is too far out of reach." If coaches and other leaders aim for low-level methods, they will get low-level results.

Most elite coaches, athletes, and organizational leaders will tell you they employ professionals. Whether these leaders' motivational actions are congruent with what they say may warrant some debate. Just what are characteristics of a professional organization? Henry Mintzberg described the professional bureaucracy orientation.[2] As such these professionals are highly trained, have a high degree of professional autonomy, have an authority derived from their expertise, and have a singular focus to the client and to their profession.

Central to any discussion of motivation theory is Abraham Maslow's seminal Needs Hierarchy.[3] The premise behind Maslow's construct is that individuals are motivated by an ever-increasing series of needs. Once one basic set of needs is met, they move up the pyramid to the next level. The most foundational needs are the basic physiological needs, then personal security and safety, followed by social affiliation. The final two levels are esteem needs, and ultimately the need for self-actualization.

Lyman Porter extended Maslow's model to fit the workplace.[4] He labeled the needs from the most basic security needs upward to affiliation, self-esteem, autonomy, and self-actualization. Frederick Herzberg then advanced a further nuanced understanding of Maslow's original work. He created a Two-Factor Theory of hygienes and motivators.[5]

In this model, the bottom three levels are not motivators; they are hygiene or maintenance factors. People can have these needs met but only sufficiently to alleviate dissatisfaction. In other words, salary and fringe benefits don't motivate people or only to a very limited degree. If these needs are not sufficiently met, then the employees may be dissatisfied. True motivation comes only from the drive to meet the upper level of Maslow's hierarchy—esteem and self-actualization.

Subsequent to these theoretical advances, Maslow refined his original needs-hierarchy.[6] Now, in ascending order, the most basic needs are physiological, then safety, then belonging and love, followed by esteem needs, cognitive, then aesthetic needs, and finally self-actualization, with transcendence occupying the top level. While not only providing a more nuanced interpretation including cognitive and aesthetic dimensions, the final model went beyond an individualized notion of self-actualization to one of collectivity or transcendence.

Finally, Michael Maccoby created his own conceptualization of motivation theory.[7] Maccoby saw the nexus between the motives of both the leader and those who are being led as critical to understanding the dimensions of motivation. In his model, leaders are motivated by either the collective good or their own personal power. Followers, on the other hand, either *have* to follow the leader or *want* to follow the leader.

This nexus is absolutely critical to determining our motivational approaches. Theory X understandings would flow from athletes or employees needing to follow and the leader chasing their own personal power. Theory Y beliefs would more likely flow from athletes and employees wanting to follow a leader who pursues the common good.

Whether adhering to Maslow's original or later work, or that of Porter, Herzberg or Maccoby, it is understood that each athlete or employee has a progressive set of needs that drive their motivation. It is the responsibility of either the boss (Theory X) or the individual (Theory Y) to address the ascending needs in order to acquire the penultimate level. An interesting question might be to consider whether it is necessary for people to have their highest esteem, autonomy, and self-actualization needs met in order for the team or organization to be successful. In either case, whose responsibility is it to move each person up the needs scale?

Do the best coaches adhere to these theoretical models of motivation? How congruent are their approaches to their beliefs? Without using the term, "Theory Y," these coaches and athletes clearly are firm believers that professionals are self-motivated, team-oriented, like challenge, and are hard-working.

Without fail, each coach and athlete stated the most important point is the need to get to know them as individuals and to build relationships and trust. They do this by listening and purposefully asking what motivates them. The best coaches show the players they value them, care about them, and are committed to them. They help their players set their own goals and standards of excellence, and then how to self-monitor. This supports them to establish a professional mindset and to develop intrinsic approaches. After all, by their very nature, elite players want to improve and be the best they can be.

These coaches help their players secure their contracts so they can support their families. They build a culture of sharing, team, and camaraderie. Both the individual and the team are empowered. It becomes a professional culture which breeds success and high expectations. This means they are treated like professionals, provided autonomy, and given flexibility in decision-making.

Former collegiate head baseball coach and star collegiate player Jon Reinebold spoke of his own experience as a team leader. "The three levers you can use for motivation are: Autonomy, Relatedness, and Competence. People are motivated by being able to make decisions on their own, by gaining competence, and by building connections and relationships."

Perhaps without even realizing it, these coaches follow Maslow's Needs Hierarchy. They make certain their team, both individually and collectively, have their most basic needs met. The athletes are safe and secure, build a camaraderie, earn a degree of self-esteem through belonging to the team and being a part of its success, and are given support to meet their own goals and expectations. When they come together and win together, they have transcended all with ultimate team success in the sense that athletics brings.

Before this portion of chapter 4 comes to closure, it would be worthwhile to examine the nature of athletics with respect to its professional-bureaucratic orientation. This will then lead seamlessly into the review of chapter 3 in the next section.

As discussed a number of times throughout this book—including earlier in this chapter—Max Weber recognized all organizations have attributes with one of four primary orientations: Professional, Bureaucratic, Weberian, or Chaotic. No organization would want to consider itself chaotic. As a matter of fact, if an organization would be characterized primarily as chaotic, it would not be around for long.

Therefore, most institutions—including athletics—would fall under one of the umbrellas of professional, bureaucratic, or Weberian. While most readers and leaders likely would profess to and want to work in a professional organization, such systems are not common. They may find themselves surrounded by professionals, but they are encumbered by structures, layers, and processes of bureaucracy. Those would be the prototypical Weberian organization. If little professional autonomy, decision-making, and entrepreneurship are permitted, the organization would likely be considered more bureaucratic.

Specifically, should athletics be considered professional, Weberian, or bureaucratic? The answer isn't as simple as the question. The larger and more complex the organization, the more likely it would be considered bureaucratic, perhaps a professional bureaucracy. The International Olympics

Committee and the U.S. Olympics Committee would certainly be considered either bureaucratic or Weberian at best. The NCAA and the professional leagues (e.g., NFL, NBA, MLB, and NHL) would also most likely be considered Weberian or even more bureaucratic.

On the other hand, individual teams and smaller unit associations might be considered either Weberian or possibly professional. In all likelihood, the leadership, owner and CEO, of the team would influence such a dynamic. Examples might include U.S. Cycling or U.S. Swimming—to name only a couple. Perhaps some DI collegiate athletic departments would most likely be indicative of Weberian models. DIII schools and certainly the individual athletic teams could show more and more signs of a professional dynamic.

The locker rooms and the "huddles" would be prime examples of a professional unit. Owners, CEOs, and even coaches spend little or no time in the locker rooms and absolutely no time in the arena of play. Those places are devoted entirely to the professionals. Those are the places where true transcendence and professionalism may take place. In the locker room and the huddle, the professionals truly do hold one another to account like no other.

Finally, the entire premise of this book is that leaders in educational and corporate institutions can learn valuable lessons from elite coaches and their athletes, particularly in the areas of leadership and motivation. If this is true, the individuals interviewed will be the ones best able to shed some light on whether or not such skills, dispositions, and attributes are transferrable.

The answer is a resounding "Yes!" The same characteristics that make coaches successful are the ones that make leaders in any organization successful. Many corporate and educational leaders, in fact, do become leaders outside athletics. Other organizations purposefully seek them out. Successful leaders, no matter the organization type, share the same intangible attributes.

These leaders are organized, practice sound time management, are self-disciplined, self-motivated, intelligent, and are experts in their fields. They are accountable, adaptable, and coachable. They approach their work and those around them with a sense of professionalism, integrity, and reliability. Without fail, they have a strong work ethic, are honest, know how to be role-players, and will step up to the challenge.

Just as importantly, they create a culture of teamwork and professionalism. They build community, team, shared goals, and responsibility, and they do this by building relationships. They are empathetic and they listen. They are role models, they are excellent communicators, and they give and earn respect. They exude persistence, grit, and selfless determination. Most of all, they let their professional teammates do their jobs—they don't need "yes men."

THE FINDINGS FROM CHAPTER 3—
ORGANIZATION FOR SUCCESS

Newtonian physics and the classical sciences have unwittingly served as the model for today's bureaucratic organizational structures. It was never Sir Isaac Newton's intention that his scientific notions would become the exemplar for our human work systems. Max Weber, concerned of too much power in one authoritarian figure, described what we have come to know as bureaucracies. Yet, he was equally worried about a system where a bureaucratic staff would eventually become too empowered. In other words, he was worried of the potential for the bureaucratic tail wagging the professional dog. Creating a system checking the power of an all-mighty autocrat at the top could be replaced with a monster of the management class.

Indeed, critical theory makes us take a step back and reflect upon what has happened to us and to our organizations. Slowly, incrementally, insidiously over time, have the professionals abdicated some of their ownership and responsibility? Have they given away not only their power but also their obligation and authority to the managing bureaucrats?

Today's classical organization was developed with efficiency, consistency, and control in mind. It is said management has five major functions: planning, organizing, commanding, coordinating, and controlling. Scientific management has truly become a science; the machine is the metaphor, and those at the top of the machine make the decisions. The governance models are depicted in Dolan's K-12 education configuration (figure 3.1) and Rettig's higher education configuration (figure 3.2).

Both of the earlier two chapters stressed the need for system leaders to understand their own values and beliefs, as well as to reflect upon what they believe about their employees. Do these leaders have a more Theory X or a Theory Y lean? Such a personal philosophy is not only critical to how leaders lead and approach motivation but so also fundamental to the way they structure their organizations. Such an orientation impacts hierarchy, communication, supervision, policies, and decision-making.

As discussed in chapter 2, a leader's view of employees characterizing more Theory X or more Theory Y attributes would impact the philosophical structure with a professional, bureaucratic, or Weberian dynamic. Chaotic organizations do not lend themselves to either Theory X or Y beliefs. However, bureaucratic structures lend themselves to a Theory X mindset and professional structures to a Theory Y mindset. Weberian structures likely support a nuanced mix of both and are the model for most of today's larger organizations.

Bureaucratic organizations are designed to provide precision across functions and employ a highly trained professional managing class with specific responsibilities and knowledge. Lines of authority and communication are clear, and decision-making is precise and not arbitrary. At least this is how bureaucracies are designed. Such systems can be confining, ignore informal structures, create low morale, stifle creativity, and produce legalism. Most importantly, the model is built on the assumption that the person on top of the pyramid knows more than those lower down in the pyramid.

Bureaucracies, further, are built with the understanding they are tightly coupled and controlled. That is, there are no competing goals, lines of communication are clear, there is no overlap in responsibilities, and formal structures and processes are the rule. Most practitioners fully realize their organizations are much more loosely coupled in reality. Communication is weak and sporadic, ambiguous goals compete with one another, workers have overlapping responsibilities, and the informal structure and processes rule the day.

Indeed, the formal and informal dichotomy impacts the work and experiences of coaches and athletes every day. For that matter, it impacts the lives of workers every day in any of our organizations. According to the coaches and their players, while their formal roles are necessary, for the most part, their greatest influence truly comes from their informal relationships with their peers and their staff. It is not either/or, it is both/and. And just as with motivation, they posit, "Be authentic—know your values and be true to yourself."

Oftentimes, the formal role and relationship are where coaches begin. Players, at first, will listen and follow the leader based on their position and their reputation. These have typically been earned by experience, expertise, intelligence, exceptional skills, and past success. The formal leader helps to establish the culture and expectations, and the formal relationships soften as one moves further down the organizational hierarchy to the assistants and to the players themselves. The formal is often considered necessary, but it is not sufficient. It can establish a baseline, but it does not move an organization to excellence.

Excellence comes from the informal structure and the informal networks and relationships. Long-term and durable success comes from within—from within the individual and from within the collective ethos. The culture is dynamic and fed by everyone within the organization. It is owned by everyone, not singularly by someone at the top.

The best coaches don't rely on their formal position of authority. At best, they use it to open the door. The work comes in the form of the everyday interaction with the professionals. It is about building trusting and caring relationships. It is about honesty and mutual development. It is personal. Such strong relationships and bonds, such an informal spirit, can only come from a Theory Y viewpoint. This cannot be harnessed and nurtured with rigid strictures.

More contemporary organizational models turn away from the classical sciences and instead look to lessons from the ecological sciences. While these scientists may see pyramids, these hierarchies are natural or organic and not rigid and fabricated. Nature is not ruled by animals or people at the top, but rather by processes that keep the entire system in check—keystone processes.

Other entrepreneurial organization thinkers look not to Newtonian Physics but to quantum physics and the other newer sciences, chaos theory, for example. These sciences indicate that at times natural systems want to maintain harmony; they seek equilibrium. At other times natural systems may move away from equilibrium as they seek innovation. Innovation and creativity are the only way they can survive—they must adapt.

These contemporary thinkers suggest our leaders need to allow for the actual underlying order to emerge from what appears to be chaos. For they believe our organizations are like living natural systems. Communication with feedback loops is the lifeblood for an organization. Systems need a process of internal checks and balances to keep the whole in balance. In order for systems to live, they must adapt, change, and create. Control might squeeze life out of the system. Small perturbations or disturbances can have a huge influence anywhere in the system. We must view the system as a whole, over time and space.

Do our coaches and athletes live in life-strangling workplaces? Are the bureaucrats running the show? The answer—"It's complicated." Much like our modern organizations, the answer is not straightforward. The bigger and the more complex the organization, the more it exhibits a bureaucratic orientation. At best, most organizations would be considered Weberian.

While most coaches and athletes find themselves ensconced within a team, the team resides within a bigger and more complex athletic department. The athletic department is nestled within a larger institution which sits within conference and NCAA hierarchies. At the professional level, the team sits within an organization which sits within a league. An Olympian toils within a sports governing body, within a national governing body, and within an international governing body. It is complicated.

At the very top of these organizational hierarchies, the system is very bureaucratic. A professional bureaucratic class runs the day-to-day operations under the direction of more or less corporate boards. The athletes and the coaches themselves do not sit on these boards or steer the organization—much akin to school boards, boards of trustees, and corporate boards.

A similar dynamic can be found within DI college athletics. These teams find heavy bureaucratic structures all around them. Smaller DIII colleges find themselves within less bureaucratic surroundings and thus find they enjoy more professional autonomy, by and large. Still, all those individuals interviewed believe that a fair balance between bureaucracy and the professional is warranted. Structure is needed that supports organic work and professional decision-makers. At times, it may be a matter of the leader's preference or style. Good leaders can adapt to their organization and to their staff or team. They don't make others adapt to them.

Many of our coaches and athletes feel the bureaucracies are becoming too heavy-handed and don't give the professionals opportunities to flourish; there is too much worry about checking the boxes, external rules, and litigation. Again, it is becoming an example of the bureaucratic tail wagging the professional dog.

Bureaucracies are said to hold people accountable, but true professionals hold themselves accountable. Elite coaches and athletes, professionals if you will, find outside accountability to be stifling and condescending, and geared toward minimal standards. They work at a higher level than the system expects. Structurally speaking, these professionals feel the model works, but it is limited when it comes to excellence. The pyramid supports and maintains stability, but excellence demands more, and professionals need more. They need more ownership, more autonomy, and more flexibility. Pyramids are not built for adaptability; they're built for stability.

Chan Gailey, for example, stated that bureaucracies in athletics are not designed for excellence.

> In pro football, the owners have been very successful in their own business models in order to have enough money to buy a team. But these business models don't always necessarily transfer to the professional football world. Coaches don't always have enough influence on drafting and trading players—but coaches are the experts. It depends on the owner—some get it.

When owners or bureaucrats don't get it, the coaches often end up serving as a buffer or a protector so that the athletes can perform as professionals without the burden of outside interference. The athletes and the coaches are ultimately the ones who must be responsible. They make decisions in both the preparations and in the actions during competition. So, while the leaders may be responsible for the overall strategy or mission, the professionals—the athletes—adjust and make decisions on the ground.

If the bureaucratic structures seem cumbersome, arcane, and stifling, how do the teams make them work? Perhaps, we need not look very far to find an exemplar for this way of thinking. Perhaps we live within such a system already—democratic governance. Our democratic values, for the sake of the workplace, would include the following: Liberty, the Common Good, Justice, Equality, Diversity, and Honesty, Openness, and Fairness. Our democratic principles are the Rule of Law, Checks and Balances, Separation of Powers, and Representative Government.

It would seem natural that our democratic values and principles follow a Theory Y philosophy. Democracy, after all, requires a learned and engaged citizenry. It certainly honors the professional and in political practice uses a Weberian approach. What do our coaches and athletes think? What kinds of system structures do they work in? Are they effective?

Again, democratic organizations are not about voting; they are about democratic values and principles. These organizations are about a culture of shared decision-making, shared responsibility, and a collective vision. This requires a safe place for the sharing of ideas, honesty, mutual respect, and challenge. Inclusion and diversity are primary. After all, ultimately, it is the professionals who have to carry out the work—they should be intimately involved in the decision-making. It is the culture.

While the coach may need to make decisions about overall strategies or plans, the players make the decisions on the field, on the court, and on the track. Such a system makes for better decisions through shared ownership, understanding, and responsibility. Everyone's role is critical to the end result.

Our organizations today are too complex for one person to make the decisions alone. They need insights and sharing from the professionals they hire. Besides, they can't make the quick decisions necessary during the game. These coaches can't afford blind loyalty or yes-men. That's not only undemocratic but ineffectual.

While shared responsibility and decision-making are most often informal, as part of the cultural and democratic ethos of successful organizations, there is an increasing awareness for the need for formal structures to guarantee participation. Professional sports now have Players Associations, and Olympic committees have Advisory Councils, as do some colleges. Even so, sometimes people need to be trained on how to make decisions, to take the responsibility, and to be democratic participants. They will then develop and hold the culture together.

PUTTING THE INTERVIEWS TOGETHER

Battles in the Trenches began by exploring general models of and approaches to institutional leadership before turning its attention to principles of motivation and organizational structure. It is time now to come full circle and hear directly from some elite coaches and athletes about their perspectives of what makes for the best leaders, and indeed, how they lead, motivate, and structure their teams.

To begin, the question was simply stated, "What do the best leaders do?" The themes emerged immediately and resoundingly across coaches and athletes alike; across college, professional, and Olympians alike; and across genders alike. The best leaders are role models, excellent communicators, and relationship builders.

Serving as stellar role models was the primary attribute of the best leaders, according to these coaches and athletes. Dick Stockton said, "It's simple—they set an example in everything they do. They are positive and walk the high ground." Mike Owensby added, "They never ask you to do something they wouldn't do themselves. They care about their people." To this point, Chan Gailey explained, "They are people of great character. Lots of people can be 'successful,' but the persons of great character are the great leaders; they find a way to help the people."

As role models, leaders must also be exceptional communicators. The best leaders are good listeners; they establish clear goals, inspire, and affirm good work, according to Gordon Marino. He added, "Good leaders have the ability to make tough decisions that people may not like—that takes courage." "They are clear in their messages and in their vision. They talk to their colleagues, not at them," according to Larry Owens. Jame Carney said they can be brutally honest but always in a caring way.

Coach Pat Cerroni was clear.

> They set the standards and make sure everyone understands them. They put the standards in writing, make them concrete, and make them relatable. Words matter. You have to know who you are, so others can know who you are. The leaders need to establish traditions. Eventually, they get the older players to become leaders—younger players today will follow the older players. These team leaders will then communicate the standards, the expectations, and the team culture.

Fred Roethlisberger added, "They are pacesetters—they model their expectations, and their actions are congruent. They are willing to do it themselves—they're teachers!" His college teammate, Barry Derickson, agreed. "The best leaders and coaches are teachers who build individual and team character." Just as important, "They know how to bring groups together and how to navigate different personalities. They're flexible, adapt, and play many different roles. They make adjustments," according to former college basketball athlete Jennifer Demby.

Former college football star Dean Green expressed,

> The best leaders lead by example. They will always lend a helping hand and they don't think they are superior to anyone. Coach Ross at the University of Maryland built relationships with the players and their families. He had a great mind of remembering details about everyone. He gained our respect, because he was successful.

Extending this line of reasoning, Gretchen Rush explicated,

These teacher-leaders help others to find motivation. They lead by example with love for the game and love for the person. They help the person with individual growth. They are masters of servant leadership. They give the people voice; they pay attention and take the time to get to get to know the individuals. They help people work together in the same direction by giving them opportunity and freedom. Team leaders acknowledge and affirm the good.

Football coach Jeff Reinebold shared an old Buddhist tenet:

Leaders "embody what they teach, and they teach only what they embody." There is the technical aspect, but at this level you can't out technical someone—that's a minor aspect. It's being congruent, to be true to the feelings—people will gladly follow someone who creates an environment that will help them grow their talents and play at the highest level. Traits are physical and straightforward, but it's the hard-to-measure attributes that are crucial.

Tavarres King said his high school coach "taught us to be a powerful and positive presence in everything we do." He added, "The best leaders lead by example. They are dedicated to a plan and follow-through with it and put others first." Joshua Pickett played football at the same high school, under a different coach—Benji Harrison, years later. Joshua explained, "The best leaders are authentic, that's when they are most powerful. They are genuine which shows their true character. In other words, they lead by example."

As role models and excellent communicators, Larry Owens noted, "A leader needs to be strong in their convictions and respect the situation and circumstances. Respect is earned. Everyone is watching the leader's reactions." How does a leader build this respect? According to Gordon Marino, "by getting to know your people, by building trust." Ann Lebedeff concurred, "It's about how you treat people. You have to understand the people you're working with. You need to have a philosophy and understand it. You need to share this philosophy with your team. Mine was 'to create good human beings.'"

It is about relationship building, according to John Roberts. He was emphatic when he noted, "Trust is the number one quality in leadership, followed by honesty." Ralston Cash has seen many good leaders. "They are understanding of you as an individual. They don't assume they know you or more than you—that they know how to treat you. The best coaches got to know us and showed respect to us." To do this, they "put the athletes first. Then they get people to work together as a team to achieve the goal," reported Jame Carney.

Jim Peeples echoed some of these same sentiments. "Great leaders want to be challenged. They know their strengths and weaknesses, stay in their lanes, and surround themselves with experts. They put people in position to excel and to work together. They have no ego." Circling back to the themes of communication along with uniting a group toward a common goal, Jon Reinebold expressed, "The best leaders develop a vision and communicate it, and they help to get others to buy into it."

In order to achieve this common goal or vision, "The best leaders surround themselves with good and smart people and let them do their jobs," according to John O'Grady. Mike Plant agreed.

> They collect people together—bring together the best people for the job that's needed. They don't worry about who gets the credit, but they take the bullets. They recognize the good work of their team. They are role-models for energy and are great motivators. They empower their team and are honest with them. Everyone knows where the leader stands—what's important to them. The leader sets the course, the vision, and allows the people to tactically execute.

Ron Stewart gave a note of advice.

> The best leaders know who they represent. For example, athletic directors represent their coaches, and coaches represent their players. Too often they are looking out for their own jobs, first. Who are they beholden to? You need to be true to who you are. Don't try to be like someone else.

Sarah Hammer added her own advice. "When you are new to a situation, don't just come in and change everything. Take the time to assess your people and the situation."

Pat Cerroni said coaches and leaders need to adapt. Coach Jamie Purdy agreed. "You need to adapt to your personnel, their age, and the environment." Mike Hartman continued,

> Our best leaders are the consummate team players. They are adaptive. They recognize the strengths in the team and minimize the weaknesses. They adapt to players' abilities, not the other way around. From my time in the military, I learned to pass credit on to the team and to accept the blame.

Finally, Abbey Dondanville said today's best leaders are democratic. "They make their people feel heard. Even if you disagree, you are comfortable in knowing you were heard—genuinely heard. And they are open to learn from others." According to Marcel Bellefeuille,

They focus on the process, not the results. Good results come from following the process. You get what you inspect or measure. You must lead with balance between the needs of the people and the process. It's transformational leadership. You transform what people think about themselves and their beliefs, and they can accomplish more.

Over the last few pages, our coaches and athletes expressed what attributes and dispositions they found to be exhibited by people they saw as excellent leaders. How do they see their own leadership or what approaches do they try to emulate?

When Gordon Marino coached boxing and football, he would spend a great deal of time with the athletes, built relationships, and learned about their personal lives. Coach Sarah Hammer said, "I am a quiet leader, not a yeller. I take the time to get to know the athletes one-on-one; that's where I make the biggest difference." Pat Cerroni is a listener, empathetic, and foremost a teacher. He explained, "Leadership is selfless. You try to help others win. You must listen and not overreact. Truly, it's about building relationships."

Jennifer Demby shared her altruistic values.

> My philosophy is to encourage a positive and respectful relationship between coach and athlete. To inspire, believe in their abilities as they grow, teach how to share, care, be kind, embrace good sportsmanship, listen, and be giving as well as forgiving. To be the best role model I can be to help our athletes build their foundation through sport and to facilitate what they learn in all aspects of their life.

In a similar vein, "I like to help and nurture people—and put them in a position to be successful and help to develop their character," Chan Gailey expressed. For John O'Grady, "I've changed over the years. When I first started out, I was more intense. Now I'm more relaxed with the players. The assistant can serve as a balance and a buffer."

Jame Carney recognizes each of his actions is being observed by the athletes and the university, so he is certain to be a role model and lead by example. Bart Andrus explained his role: "I'm an informative leader. The team needs as much information as possible. Communication both ways is key. We all have to be on the same page." Harry Sydney added, "You do your job and helps others do theirs. You help other people understand the common goal. You communicate. It has to make sense to them, and then you have to act on it!"

As a military commander, Jon Reinebold would communicate to his soldiers and staff, "This is how your behavior or actions are going to affect the military. That's an example of attacking the problem not the person." He added, "When you fail to enforce a standard, you set a new standard." Coach Reinebold extended those lessons to his team at the college level.

As a college AD Darryl Sims expressed his approach:

> I hire the best people I can. I research the individual to find people who are: 1) self-motivated, 2) self-starters, 3) who can make tough decisions, 4) and loyal to self, to me, the department, and the campus. They need to fit in and support our culture, have strong integrity, and be trustworthy. In turn, I give them support to do their job and make their decisions as professionals. The best ADs let the coaches run their programs and don't micromanage. I give them the resources they "need" not necessarily "want."

Coach Marcel Bellefeuille knows his work is about building culture. His work is transformational. Nicky Bowman always relates back to her roots as a Native American. Her leadership approach is distributive and flows through her ancestors and into future generations. In this way, her leadership is circular.

Coach Jamie Purdy reflected,

> Morals and core values are the foundation for my decisions. It's more than just the game. Sometimes I have to go into "Mom-mode" where I am not coaching, but I'm nurturing, listening, caring, and building relationships. Early in my career it was about my love of the game and competing. It's still that, but it's much more about the relationships.

Athletic director and former college coach Jim Peeples concluded,

> First and foremost, I'm a servant leader. Too many leaders think the people serve them, but we need to serve the people. Bad leaders leave their employees feeling empty and unmotivated. I'm here to support those around me; it is critical to have good role models.

These coaches' and players' stories, when pulled together in a unifying whole, create a mosaic of undeniable clarity. Both individually and collectively, they have been successful in their careers. They have been extraordinarily reflective and candid, and they serve as tremendous exemplars for future leaders, not only in the field of athletics but also in the fields of K-12 and higher education, and certainly in corporate America.

It all begins with their belief in people. They believe athletes and employees actually appreciate work, are team-oriented, goal-driven, self-motivated, and most of all, professional. Our coaches and athletes are Theory Y proponents.

They have faith in people. They build relationships and help their teams build relationships with one another. A transformational culture is the path, and collective team empowerment and shared democratic processes are the vehicle. These leaders build, they adapt, and they support professionalism. These servant leaders lead—their organizations are transcendent.

PULLING THE MODELS TOGETHER

It is now time to put the leadership, motivational, and structural mosaic together in a manner that makes sense. More to the point, if you believe most employees fall into a Theory X frame, then what motivation approaches would you use with them? What would be the organizational structure you would use to manage or lead them?

Conversely, if you are a proponent of Theory Y, how would you approach leadership and motivation with your employees, and what organizational structure would best help you reach your ends? To do this, Rettig has developed a crosswalk linking leadership theory with motivation theory with organizational theory, all under the umbrellas of Theories X and Y. For lack of a better term, he has called this, "Congruence Modeling."[8]

Neither a coach nor a college president would be served well, for example, if they believe people are lazy and indolent, yet they were forced to use an intrinsic motivation model coupled with a democratic decision-making process. At the same time, any leader would feel incongruent if they believed people were professional and hard-working, yet they were forced into an autocratic structure with extrinsic motivation expectations placed upon them.

Leaders who believe most employees are lazy, unmotivated, need to be told what to do, and must be carefully supervised, would follow a Theory X model. These types of employees, by their very nature, would need a traditional top-down authoritative boss or coach who would tell them the expectations and then closely monitor their progress toward meeting those expectations. Such a leader would be responsible for providing external motivation and use a tightly coupled hierarchical structure.

Leaders who believe, on the other hand, employees take pride in their work are self-motivated, hard-working, and enjoy working as a team, would follow a Theory Y inclination. These types of employees would better excel in a more professional and informal or loosely coupled structure where democratic and organic decision-making is the norm. A leader would be responsible for keeping the organization's mission and values central to all conversations and to help establish a culture where intrinsic or self-motivation can be expressed.

Putting these principles and approaches to leadership, motivation, and organizational structure together into a singular model can help leaders

Theory X	Theory Y
Leadership Approach	*Leadership Approach*
Transactional/Authoritarian/Autocratic	Transformational/Democratic/Servant
More Formal	More Informal
Manipulative/Calculating/Fear	Love/Respect/Culture-building
Power	*Power*
Authority from Position/Legitimate	Authority from Values/Service/Virtues
Power Over	Power Through
Management Orientation	Professional Orientation
Motivation	*Motivation*
External/Extrinsic	Internal/Intrinsic
Leader owns responsibility	People own responsibility
Lower level Maslow	Upper level Maslow
Herzberg Hygienes	Herzberg Motivators
Organizational Model	*Organizational Model*
Traditional Pyramid Hierarchy	Ecological or Democratic principles
Bureaucratic Orientation	Professional Orientation
Tightly Coupled—formal	Loosely Coupled—informal
Machine Metaphor	*Natural Metaphor*

Figure 4.1 Leadership Congruency Model.

establish congruency of their beliefs with the practices they follow. (See figure 4.1 Leadership Congruency Model). The leadership approach, the motivation approach, and the organizational structure should all flow from your belief about people, vis-à-vis, Theory X or Theory Y.

When a leader finds that the beliefs of employees are not supported by approaches, system policies, and structures, there will be an incongruence. Such an incongruence can lead to low morale and frustration on the part of both the leader and the employees and certainly can lead to a dysfunctional or less-than-optimal work environment.

The Leadership Congruency Model (figure 4.1) aligns leadership approaches and their views of power or authority, motivational approaches, and organizational structures together within a philosophical framework of how leaders view their employees—Theory X or Theory Y.

*Laissez-faire doesn't seem to fit either, neither does chaotic. Coaching and pacesetting can fit either.

For example, if the leader believes their employees or team are lazy, indolent, unmotivated, recalcitrant, and just want to punch the clock, they would hold Theory X beliefs. Such a team or a system would need a leader who is autocratic or authoritarian, a boss if you will, and uses transactional approaches. They would rely on formal positional authority and need to cajole players or staff to meet the expectations the supervisors have established. The bosses expect and then inspect.

As such, it is the leader who is responsible for goal achievement and employee motivation. Their focus is on rewarding and coercing their colleagues via more basic need levels of Maslow and Herzberg. To accomplish these tasks, the leader would utilize the traditional bureaucratic pyramid model to best assure standardization. Indeed, the factory or machine would serve as their model.

If on the other hand, the leader was to hold a Theory Y belief system—in other words, they felt their employees are self-motivated, goal-oriented, hard workers, team-oriented, and professional—they would prefer a more natural metaphor. Realizing their ultimate power in working with professionals comes from shared values and beliefs, these leaders more likely espouse servant leadership qualities and hold a transformative cultural ethos.

To be congruent with these beliefs, the Theory Y leader would support their team's and colleagues' intrinsic motivational drives. Their focus would support self-actualized momentum; indeed, it would coalesce around a collective transcendency. Such a model would require a democratic and professional structure encouraging informal leadership within and across the organization. Both power and culture would be shared by all.

Of course, few people would consider themselves so purely one or the other. They would say some of their employees exhibit more Theory X or Y attributes than others. Most administrators would follow a mixed situational approach. Few organizations are wholly formally structured, realizing the existence of an informal system, too. In fact, many of our organizations have some degree of a professional-bureaucratic blend, resembling a Weberian model.

Nevertheless, each leader has a preferred belief and model in mind, and each organization would certainly lean more toward a professional or a bureaucratic structure. The leadership imperative—actions, processes, and structures—must be congruent with beliefs. Such is the call for all leaders.

CODA

Like all theories, the Leadership Congruency Model is a generalized construct developed in its purest form. People, their idiosyncrasies, and the organizations in which they work are not so pure or academic. Life is complex. None of us work in wholly congruent organizations, and none of the people we lead fall cleanly into one theory or another. Similarly, no organization is either completely professional or bureaucratic. We live in a gray world. However, our values should be clear to us, and we should endeavor to lead, to approach motivation, and to structure our organizations in a way that is congruent with our espoused values and beliefs about the people we lead.

It would be very worth your time to reflect on your beliefs about people. Are you more aligned with Theory X or Y thinking? Are your leadership approaches congruent with these beliefs? Are your approaches to employee motivation subsequently congruent? Finally, are your organization and policies structured to best support your values and beliefs?

What attributes of these successful athletes and coaches do you share? Which lessons can you begin to implement? Can you make your organization more democratic by supporting more democratic values and principles? What would a more organic and informal structure look like? How would it be possible to create a transcendent organization and to become a transformational leader?

NOTES

1. John Kotter, *What Leaders Really Do* (Cambridge, MA: Harvard Business School Press, 1999).

2. Henry Mintzberg, *The Structuring of Organizations* (Englewood Cliffs, NJ: Prentice-Hall, 1978).

3. Abraham Maslow, *Religions, Values, and Peak Experiences* (New York: Penguin, 1970).

4. Lyman Porter, "A Study of Perceived Need Satisfaction in Bottom and Middle-Management Jobs." *Journal of Applied Psychology* 45 (1961): 1–10.

5. Frederick Herzberg, *Work and the Nature of Man* (Cleveland, OH: World Publishing, 1966), 56.

6. Abraham Maslow in Saul McLeod, "Maslow's Hierarchy of Needs," *Simply Psychology*, (March 20, 2020), https://www.simplypsychology.org/maslow.html.

7. Michael Maccoby, *The Leaders We Need and What Makes Us Follow* (Boston, MA: Harvard Business School Press, 2007).

8. Perry Rettig and Darryl Sims, *Battles in the Trenches: How Leaders in Academia, Elite Athletes, and Coaches Can Learn from Each Other* (Lanham, MD: Rowman & Littlefield, 2022).

This is the first time the *Leadership Congruency Model* has appeared in print and was created by Perry Rettig.

The chart in figure 4.1 shows how different leadership approaches or styles best mesh with the appropriate motivation principles, as well as organizational structures, all flowing from the *ab initio* belief in people as Theory X or Theory Y.

Bibliography

Capra, Fritjof and Pier Luigi Luisi. *The Systems View of Life: A Unifying Vision.* Cambridge: Cambridge University Press, 2014.

Carroll, Sean B. *The Serengeti Rules.* Princeton, NJ: Princeton University Press, 2016. "The Serengeti Rules." *Nature.* Video of the Public Broadcasting System. Edited by Benedict Jackson. Executive Producer: David Guy Elisco, Jared Lipworth, and Fred Kaufman. Produced by David Allen and Gaby Bastyra. October 9, 2019. Based on the book by Sean B. Carroll. The Serengeti Rules. Princeton, NJ: Princeton University Press, 2016.

Cerroni, Pat. PowerPoint. "Target," University of Wisconsin Oshkosh. *Fall Leadership 2021*, 2021.

Dolan, Patrick. *Restructuring Our Schools: A Primer on Systemic Change.* Kansas City: Systems & Organization, 1994.

"Five Types of Leadership Styles in Management," https://emplify.com/blog/5-types-of-leadership-styles-in-management/.

Glickman, Carl, Stephen Gordon, and Jovita Ross-Gordon. *Supervision of Instruction A Developmental Approach.* Boston, MA: Allyn & Bacon, 1998.

Goleman, Daniel. *Emotional Intelligence: Why it can Matter More than IQ.* New York: Random House Publishing Group, 2005.

Goleman, Daniel. "Leadership that gets Results." *Harvard Business Review,* 78–90 (March 2000).

Haden, Karl and Rob Jenkins. *The 9 Virtues of Exceptional Leaders: Unlocking Your Leadership Potential.* Atlanta, GA: Deeds Publishing, 2015.

Hersey, Paul and Kenneth Blanchard. *Management and Organizational Behavior: Utilizing Human Resources.* Englewood Cliffs, NJ: Prentice Hall, 1969.

Herzberg, Frederick. *Work and the Nature of Man.* Cleveland, OH: World Publishing, 1966, 56.

Jackson, Jesse. Paraphrased Speech to Students at the University of Wisconsin Oshkosh—Paraphrased by Perry R. Rettig, March 28, 2011.

Jenkins, Sally. "Keys to Good Coaching," article in the Washington Post. Carried in the *Atlanta Journal Constitution* (December 26, 2021), 42.

Kotter, John. *What Leaders Really Do.* Cambridge, MA: Harvard Business School Press, 1999.

"Leadership Styles: Learn the 7 Different Management Styles." https://leaders.com/articles/leadership/leadership-styles.

Lombardi, Vince and W. C. Heinz. *Run to Daylight.* New York: Prentice Hall, 1967.

Luft, Joseph. *Group Processes: An Introduction to Group Dynamics.* New York: National Press Books, 1970.

Maccoby, Michael. *The Leaders We Need and What Makes Us Follow.* Boston, MA: Harvard Business School Press, 2007.

Machiavelli, Niccolo. *The Prince.* Translated by Ninian Hill Thomson. SDE Classics Philosophy Collection, 2019.

Maraniss, David. *When Pride Still Mattered: A Life of Vince Lombardi.* New York: Simon & Schuster, 1999.

Maslow, Abraham. *Religions, Values, and Peak Experiences.* New York: Penguin, 1970.

McGregor, Douglas. *The Human Side of Enterprise.* New York: McGraw-Hill, 1960.

McLeod, Saul. "Maslow's Hierarchy of Needs." *Simply Psychology* (March 20, 2020). https://www.simplypsychology.org/maslow.html.

Mintzberg, Henry. *The Structuring of Organizations.* Englewood Cliffs, NJ: Prentice-Hall, 1978.

Northouse, Peter G. *Leadership: Theory and Practice.* 5th edition. Los Angeles, CA: Sage, 2010.

Olson, Gary. "Exactly What is 'Shared Governance'?" *The Chronicle of Higher Education* (July 23, 2009).

Owens, Robert. *Organizational Behavior in Education: Adaptive Leadership and School Reform.* Boston: Pearson, Allyn & Bacon, 2004.

Porter, Lyman. "A Study of Perceived Need Satisfaction in Bottom and Middle-Management Jobs." *Journal of Applied Psychology* 45 (1961): 1–10.

Prigogine, Ilya and Isabelle Stengers. *Order Out of Chaos.* New York: Bantam Books, 1984, 307.

Rettig, Perry R. *Making Shared Governance Meaningful.* Lanham, MD: Rowman & Littlefield, 2020.

Rettig, Perry. "Taking His Hits with Playing Semi-Pro Football." Article in the *Atlanta Journal Constitution* (February 3, 2020), A5.

Rettig, Perry R. *The Quantum University: New Knowledge Requires New Thinking.* Lanham, MD: Rowman & Littlefield, 2021.

Satinover, Jeffrey. *The Quantum Brain: The Search for Freedom and the Next Generation of Man.* New York: John Wiley & Sons, 2002, 203.

Sergiovanni, Thomas. *Value-Added Leadership: How to get Extraordinary Performance in Schools.* New York: Harcourt, Brace, Jovanovich Publishers, 1990.

Sergiovanni, Thomas and Robert Starratt. *Supervision: A Redefinition.* New York: McGraw-Hill, 1993.

Spears, Larry. August 1998 in the Preface xix-xx to Robert K. Greenleaf's, *The Power of Servant Leadership.* Edited by Larry C. Spears. San Francisco, CA: Berrett-Koehler Publishers, Inc., 1998.

"Ten Common Leadership Styles." Indeed Editorial Team. June 30, 2021. https://www.indeed.com/career-advice/career-development/10-common-leadership-styles.

"Ten Different Types of Leadership Styles," https://online.norwich.edu/academic-programs/resources/10-different-types-leadership-styles.

Waldrop, Michael. *Complexity: The Emerging Science at the Edge of Order and Chaos*. New York: Simon & Schuster, 1992, 11.

Weick, Karl. "Educational Organizations as Loosely Coupled Systems." *Administrative Science Quarterly* 21 (1976): 1–19.

Wheatley, Margaret. *Leadership and the New Science: Learning about Organizations from an Orderly Universe*. San Francisco: Berrett-Koehler, 1994.

Wills, Garry. *Certain Trumpets: The Nature of Leadership*. New York: Simon & Schuster, 1995.

"What are the 7 Types of Leadership Styles?" https://www.mvorganizing.org/what-are-the-7-types-of-leadership-styles/. [Each of these websites were accessed on July 30, 2021].

Biographies

Bart Andrus—Andrus is current head coach for the new USFL Philadelphia Stars. He is the former head coach for NFL Europe Amsterdam and CFL Toronto and was an assistant coach for NFL Tennessee and St. Louis. Collegiately, he played quarterback and punter at the University of Montana.

Marcel Bellefeuille—Bellefeuille is head football coach and national champion at the University of Ottawa. He is a former head coach for Hamilton of the CFL and held roles as an offensive coordinator/positional coach with Montreal, BC, Winnipeg, Saskatchewan, among others, during his twenty years of professional experience. Coach Bellefeuille is also an author and keynote speaker.

Nicky Bowman—Bowman holds a doctorate in Multijurisdictional Policy, Leadership, and Governance from the University of Wisconsin. She is in the National Women's Outdoor Volleyball Hall of Fame—participated in Olympic trials and competed nationally on the USA Volleyball team and as a National Women's Natural Bodybuilder.

Marcus Campbell—Campbell played football collegiately at LaGrange College. He was named two-time all-conference as a wide receiver. Campbell played in the All-American Bowl and the Tazon Azteca Bowl. He majored in Marketing and Entrepreneurship and minored in History.

Jame Carney—Carney is a former Olympian and professional cyclist. He is a three-time Olympian (athlete and coach) with fifth place finish in 2000 Sydney. Currently, he serves as cycling head coach at Piedmont University. Carney is a two-time World Cup Champion and served on the USA Cycling board of directors and the USOPC Athlete Advisory Council from 2012 to 2016.

Ralston Cash—Cash was drafted as a pitcher by the Los Angeles Dodgers in 2010. He played in the minor league for the Dodgers, Mariners, and Orioles. He started a foundation for children with cancer: Facebook.com/RalstonCash Foundation.

Pat Cerroni—Cerroni is former head coach at DIII University of Wisconsin Oshkosh football. His 2016 team played in the national championship game. He is a veteran of the U.S. Air Force. Cerroni played his freshman year at Carroll University in Waukesha, Wisconsin. His "Championship Target" is appended to this book.

Jennifer Demby—Demby played on the 1996 U.S. Olympic handball team and the 1995 Pan-American gold medal team. She played college basketball at the University of Massachusetts Lowell. Demby currently serves as an adjunct instructor at Rutgers University and at a center for the blind and is cofounder, coach, and director of Sports of Blind Athletes Inc.

Barry Derickson—Derickson is head coach for Sul Ross State University in Texas. He is a former tight ends coach at Valparaiso University and has coached at Howard Payne, Bemidji State, Eastern Kentucky, Angelo State, and the University of Wisconsin Stevens Point. Derickson played offensive tackle for the University of Wisconsin Oshkosh.

Abbey Dondanville—Dondanville played rugby at St. Andrews University and currently competes at the Olympic level as an equestrian rider as a member of the U.S. Equestrian Federation and the Federation Equestrian International. She also serves as professor and associate dean in the College of Nursing and Health Sciences at Piedmont University.

Chan Gailey—Gailey is former NFL head coach for Dallas and Buffalo and for Georgia Tech. University. He played collegiately as quarterback at the University of Florida. Gailey was an assistant NFL Coach in Miami, Kansas City, New York, Denver, and Pittsburgh, and coached in NFL Europe.

Willie Garrett—Garrett walked on at Nebraska football as a freshman. He transferred to Midland University (NAIA) in Nebraska as a running back and subsequently tried out for Minnesota in the NFL. He has served as head coach in the Women's LFL—Omaha and Las Vegas. Garrett is the marketing director at KSNV television in Las Vegas.

Dean Green—Green played wide receiver and free safety at the University of Maryland. Green was a high school All-American. His son, Juwan Green, plays in the NFL. Dean is a retired law enforcement officer and now lives in Las Vegas.

Juwan Green—Green has played wide receiver in the NFL for both Atlanta and Detroit and is currently a free agent. He graduated from the university at Albany Stare University in New York and set several school records. He majored in communications with a minor in history.

Burke Griffin—Griffin played DIII football and was captain at the University of Wisconsin Oshkosh, where he also wrestled. He is currently sports director and anchor at WFRV Television in Green Bay, Wisconsin. Griffin covers the Packers in his "Locker Room" program.

Sarah Hammer—Hammer is a former professional and Olympic women's cyclist. She is a three-time Olympian and has won four Silver Olympic medals and fourteen World Champion medals, and Gold and Silver medals at the Pan American Games. She currently holds the world record in the 3,000-meter individual pursuit. Hammer is a U.S. paralympics coach and associate director.

Mike Hartman—Hartman played football at Central Missouri State University and then lacrosse at the University of Wisconsin LaCrosse. He played for, coached, and owned a semi-pro football team—the Fox Valley Force in Wisconsin. Hartman currently resides in Florida.

Tavarres King—King played wide receiver in the NFL from 2013 to 2018. He was drafted by Denver and also played with Carolina, Jacksonville, Tampa Bay, New York Giants, and Minnesota. King attended and played collegiately at the University of Georgia.

Ann Lebedeff—Lebedeff is head coach for the women's tennis team at Pomona-Pitzer Colleges. Her highest ranking was #6 in women's doubles, and she won numerous national championships in doubles. Lebedeff is a member of the Intercollegiate Tennis Hall of Fame.

Gordon Marino—Marino attended the University of Chicago. He serves as the Soren Kierkegaard professor at St. Olaf University. Marino is a USA amateur and professional boxing coach (who oversees USA Olympic boxing coaches) and was an assistant football coach at Yale. He also is a boxing writer for the *Wall Street Journal*.

Evan Oglesby—Oglesby played cornerback at DII University of Northern Alabama. He played six years in the NFL with Buffalo, Baltimore, Dallas, and Miami. Presently, Oglesby runs the Evan Oglesby Foundation: www.evanoglesbyfoundation.org

John O'Grady—O'Grady is the former football head coach at the University of Wisconsin River Falls. He also played at UW River Falls as linebacker and was selected as team captain. He currently is special teams coordinator at UW Whitewater. O'Grady has also coached at UW Oshkosh and UW Stout, with four years at Wisconsin, two years at Kent State, and two years at Miami of Ohio.

Larry Owens—Owens attended Cal State Fullerton. He began as a high school coach and then served as assistant coach at San Mateo College before becoming defensive line coach at Humboldt State University. Owens later returned to San Mateo to become head coach. He also served as defensive coordinator in NFL Europe Amersterdam.

Mike Owensby—Owensby walked on as a defensive lineman at Middle Tennessee State University. After working in corporate America, he became a high school science teacher and head golf coach in the state of Georgia. Owensby is a Woodrow Wilson Scholar.

Jim Peeples—Peeples played both football and baseball at Westminster College in Pennsylvania. He served as head baseball coach at Piedmont University north of Atlanta, Georgia and presently serves as athletic director at Piedmont.

Joshua Pickett—Pickett currently plays cornerback for Duke University. Joshua is studying Psychology and Business Marketing and Management. He is a multiple-sport athlete having played high school football, basketball, and track, and lettered in each sport each year played.

Mike Plant—Plant is president and CEO of Atlanta Braves Development and former executive vice president at Turner Sports. Plant was a USA Olympic speedskater and member of the U.S. World speedskating team. He has served on many committees and boards for the U.S. Olympic Committee (USOC), U.S. Speedskating, International Cycling Federation, and USA Cycling.

Jamie Purdy—Purdy played and coached women's basketball at Piedmont University and serves as assistant athletic director. She continues as head coach at Piedmont for over eighteen years and two years prior at Middle Georgia College. Purdy also played college softball.

Jeff Reinebold—Reinebold played running back in college for the University of Maine. He became head coach at Rocky Mountain College for one year and head coach at CFL Winnipeg. He also served as assistant coach and coordinator in NFL Europe—Rhein and Amsterdam, CFL—British Columbia, Edmonton, Montreal, and Hamilton and at numerous colleges including Hawaii, Louisiana Tech, SMU, and New Mexico.

Jon Reinebold—Reinebold is a former baseball second baseman at West Point. He is a retired special operations aviator, and aviation battalion commander in Japan. Reinebold has served as assistant coach at both West Point and USMMA.

John Roberts—Roberts played rugby at the University of South Carolina. He coached for twenty years at Furman University and presently serves as head rugby coach at the USC. He has coached three DIII national championship teams and a DII national championship finalist. Roberts also served as associate vice president for Marketing at Piedmont University.

Fred Roethlisberger—Roethlisberger is agency coowner of Symmetry Financial Group in Houston, Texas. He played linebacker and defensive line for DII Northern Michigan University and DIII University of Wisconsin Oshkosh. Roethlisberger was an All-State Defense Player in high school in the State of Michigan.

Gretchen Rush—Rush played collegiately at Trinity University and is in the Women's Collegiate Tennis Hall of Fame. She played on the 1984 U.S. Olympic team and played professionally at Wimbledon, the U.S. Open, the French Open, and the Australian Open. Her highest ranking was #22. Rush has coached at Trinity University and now serves at Hollins University.

Darryl Sims—played defensive tackle for the University of Wisconsin in the early 1980s. He then played in the NFL for Pittsburg and Cleveland. After his professional playing career ended, Sims coached in NFL Europe Amsterdam, Cologne, and Berlin. He then coached in the NFL for Oakland. He currently serves as athletic director and assistant chancellor at the University of Wisconsin Oshkosh and has served on several NCAA committees.

Gabby Smith Roethlisberger—Smith Roethlisberger is the coowner and branch manager of Symmetry Financial Group in Houston, Texas. She played pitcher and outfield collegiately for the softball team at the University of Texas.

Ron Stewart—Stewart is a scout for NBA Milwaukee. He is the former head coach of women's basketball for eleven seasons at Western Michigan University. Stewart was an assistant coach at the University of Florida and at the University of Nevada at Reno.

Dick Stockton—Stockton played tennis collegiately at Trinity University. His highest world ranking was #8. Stockton played in the Olympics, Wimbledon, U.S. Davis Cup, U.S. Open, and French Open. He retired as head tennis coach at the University of Virginia and then Piedmont University.

Harry Sydney—Sydney played running back at the University of Kansas and then for six years with NFL San Francisco and Green Bay. He also coached for the Packers and has three Super Bowl rings as player and coach. Sydney now leads *My Brothers' Keeper* in Green Bay. www.mybrotherskeeperinc.net.

About the Authors

Perry Rettig is distinguished university professor at Piedmont University north of Atlanta, Georgia. He has been an educator for thirty-nine years serving most recently as vice president at Piedmont. *Battles in the Trenches* is his eighth book with Rowman & Littlefield. Beyond his book publications and teaching expectations, Rettig has published dozens of professional journal articles as well as newspaper articles. He has presented papers many times over to international and national audiences. His work focuses primarily on leadership and higher education governance.

Darryl Sims played defensive tackle for the University of Wisconsin in the early 1980s. He then played in the NFL for Pittsburg and Cleveland. After his professional playing career ended, Sims coached in NFL Europe Amsterdam, Cologne, and Berlin. He then coached in the NFL for Oakland. He currently serves as athletic director and assistant chancellor at the University of Wisconsin Oshkosh and has served on several NCAA committees including Interpretation and Legislation, Name Image and Likeness, and New Constitution.

www.ingramcontent.com/pod-product-compliance
Lightning Source LLC
Chambersburg PA
CBHW030122240426
43673CB00041B/1371